Karel Husa, 1986. Photograph by Charles Harrington. *Courtesy of Cornell University.*

KAREL HUSA

KAREL HUSA

A Bio-Bibliography

Susan Hayes Hitchens

Bio-Bibliographies in Music, Number 31
Donald L. Hixon, Series Adviser

Greenwood Press
New York • Westport, Connecticut • London

Library of Congress Cataloging-in-Publication Data

Hitchens, Susan Hayes.
    Karel Husa : a bio-bibliography / Susan Hayes Hitchens.
       p.   cm. — (Bio-bibliographies in music, ISSN 0742-6968 ; no. 31)
    Includes bibliographical references and index.
    ISBN 0-313-25585-7 (alk. paper)
    1. Husa, Karel, 1921- —Bibliography. 2. Husa, Karel, 1921- —Discography. I. Title. II. Series.
    ML134.H93H57 1991
    016.78'092—dc20   90-20133

British Library Cataloguing in Publication Data is available.

Library of Congress Catalog Card Number: 90-20133
ISBN: 0-313-25585-7
ISSN: 0742-6968

First published in 1991

Greenwood Press, 88 Post Road West, Westport, CT 06881
An imprint of Greenwood Publishing Group, Inc.

Printed in the United States of America

The paper used in this book complies with the Permanent Paper Standard issued by the National Information Standards Organization (Z39.48-1984).

10 9 8 7 6 5 4 3 2 1

Contents

Preface

Karel Husa, American composer, conductor and educator of Czechoslovakian origin, is an eminent contributor to modern musical literature, especially well known for his compositions for wind band. His services as guest conductor and lecturer are in constant demand throughout the musical world. This book is intended to provide a guide to his compositions and recordings, together with a comprehensive survey of the writings about Husa and his work. Consistent with other volumes in the Greenwood Press *Bio-Bibliographies in Music* series, the text is divided into four major sections:

1. A brief biography, constructed from an interview with Professor Husa, with the assistance of Donald M. McLaurin's impressive study of Husa's music: *The life and works of Karel Husa with emphasis on the contribution to the wind band* (see B19);

2. A complete list of Husa's compositions, arranged by genre. Each work is assigned a "work" number (e.g. W1, W2, W3, etc.); the entry for each work includes the date of composition, duration, specific performance medium, and information on the commission, premiere and publication, as well as any other pertinant data;

3. A discography of commercially produced sound recordings of Husa's music, arranged alphabetically by title. Each citation is assigned a "discography" number (e.g. D1, D2, etc.) and includes the manufacturer's label and label number, date of issue, contents and performers;

4. A comprehensive bibliography of writings by or about Husa. This section is arranged alphabetically by author, or by title in cases where no author is cited. Each citation is assigned a "bibliography" number (e.g. B1, B2, etc.) and includes a short annotation and/or quotation.

Each section of the book is cross-referenced with the others; with the exception of the biography, detailed information about the section is included at the head of each division.

Two appendices are provided: lists of Husa's compositions, arranged alphabetically by title and chronologically by date of composition.

An index, including subjects and personal, corporate and geographical names is included at the end of the volume.

Acknowledgments

I would like to thank many persons who provided essential assistance, support and encouragement during the preparation of this volume:

Marilyn Clark, Reference Librarian, University of Kansas Libraries (for assistance with Czech translations); Barbara Jones, Reference Librarian, University of Kansas Libraries (for data base searching assistance); Sandra Brandt and the entire staff of the Interlibrary Loan Department of the University of Kansas Libraries; John Miller, Systems Librarian, University of Kansas Libraries (for microcomputing assistance); Gaile Burchill, Secretary, Anschutz Science Library, University of Kansas (for printing assistance); Mary Hawkins, Assistant Dean for Public Services, University of Kansas Libraries; George Woodyard, Associate Vice Chancellor for Academic Affairs, University of Kansas; Betty Birdseye, Music Librarian, Ithaca College; Lenore Coral, Music Librarian, Cornell University; Sue Sackman, Program Office Assistant, The Cleveland Orchestra; Hana Yoffe, Detroit Symphony Orchestra Librarian; Susan Wade, Public Relations, Chicago Symphony Orchestra; Elizabeth Smart Runyon, Publications Director, Cincinnati Symphony Orchestra; Eleanor McGourty, Program Office, Boston Symphony Orchestra; Jules Kovach, principal Music Librarian and Archivist, Buffalo Philharmonic Orchestra; Ann Unger, Administrative Services Director, Kansas City Symphony.

I would also like to thank Kaia Skaggs and Jerree Catlin, Academic Computing Services, University of Kansas, for processing and microcomputing assistance.

I also thank my brother, Ralph M. Hitchens, for his microcomputing assistance, and my parents, Harold L. and Marilyn B. Hitchens, for editorial assistance.

I am grateful to Dorman Smith, Music Librarian, University of Arizona, for providing editorial assistance.

Donald Hixon, general editor of the series, provided much needed support and encouragement, as well as editorial assistance.

Finally, I am most grateful to Professor Karel Husa for the generous assistance and support he has given me during the preparation of this book. His cooperation and enthusiasm have been extremely encouraging and helpful, and must be acknowledged as indispensable in the completion of this project.

KAREL HUSA

Biography

Karel Husa, born in Prague, Czechoslovakia on August 17, 1921, is the older of
two children born to Karel Husa, Sr., and Božena Dongresová-Husová. His
childhood was spent in a middle-class neighborhood of Prague, and his formal
education began when he started to attend a local elementary school in 1927. His
father supervised shoemaking in a company, comprised of World War I veterans,
which made prostheses and regular shoes.

Although both of his parents, and especially his mother, wanted their son to
become an engineer, they also insisted that he and his sister learn to play a
musical instrument. When he received a half-size violin as a Christmas gift in
1929, his mother arranged for him to take lessons with a violinist, trained in
Leningrad, who lived near the Husa family. His teacher, Antonín Švejnoha,
immediately advised the family to exchange the half-size instrument for a
full-sized violin, and his lessons began. Although the family income was
somewhat lower than average, Husa began with two lessons each week,
consisting of one-half hour of private instruction, and one and one-half to two
hours of music copying. (In order to keep expenses at the lowest possible level,
his teacher supervised Husa in copying the music he would later be studying.[1])
In the following year, the family purchased an upright piano, and his sister began
taking private piano lessons twice a week as well, from the wife of Husa's violin
teacher. Four private music lessons a week were a significant financial sacrifice
for the Husa family, but the parents deemed it important that both children
receive a musical education.

> For my mother, there was sport, there was work, but art was
> something she didn't understand but admired very much. Her
> dream was for my sister to play the piano and go to the
> Conservatory. Music was an avocation for me, but my sister was to
> become a pianist.[2]

From the beginning, the young violinist received praise and support from his mother. Her encouragement was a strong inspiration for Husa, and his interest in music and command of his instrument grew constantly under the rigorous instruction of Švejnoha.

Deferring to his parent's wishes that he study to become an engineer, in the fall of 1932 Husa entered the Státní reálka, a preparatory school for the engineering academy Vysoká škola technická. He specialized in mathematics and engineering, and, inspired by his early engineering studies in drawing, drafting and calligraphy, began to study painting with a young painter living near the Husas. During this time, he continued his violin studies, and his teacher soon considered his technical abilities to be consistent with early Conservatory-level study. Švejnoha requested that Husa apply for permission to enter the Conservatory, but Karel, Sr., refused, declaring again that his son was to be an engineer.[3]

In 1934, Karel, Sr., bought the shoe store from the company in which he worked, and Husa and his sister began to work in the store. As the family business grew, Husa's workload of pre-engineering studies at the Státní reálka increased, and so he decided to suspend his violin studies at this time. This, however, was only a brief intermission for his musical education.

The German occupation of Czechoslovakia began in the spring of 1939, just prior to Husa's graduation from the Reálka. After graduation, he immediately entered the Vysoká škola technická, but the Nazis closed the school at the end of the fall term, in order to quiet protests over a shooting incident in which a student was killed. At this time, Husa was drafted to work in a factory in Dresden, but simply never reported. Upon receiving a warning that he must report to the Nazi labor office, he sought and was granted an exemption from the draft, as he was working in the family business. "It was incredible luck; I just didn't go to Germany."[4]

During this time, he applied for admission to the Art Academy, and was accepted. However, he was required to declare that he had not previously attended the Vysoká škola technická, and rather than risk being sent to a concentration camp or prison by falsifying his application, Husa decided not to attend the Academy, and remained at home, working with his father.

Husa was introduced to Váša Černý, the principal cellist of the Prague Philharmonic, in early 1940. When Černý learned of Husa's musical background, he arranged for concert tickets to be made available to Husa, and eventually requested that Husa play for him. Černý indicated that although Husa's playing was rusty, he had a good technique, and arranged for Husa to meet Jaroslav Řídký, who lived near the Husas and taught composition at the Prague Conservatory. Confident that Řídký would be impressed, Husa brought him some early compositions (performed only for family and friends, and not known to exist today). Although Řídký did not comment on the compositions, he was impressed with Husa's ear, and accepted him as a private student, arranging for him to study harmony as well as ear training.

Řídký didn't really think anything of these compositions. Later, I would hear him frequently say to a student, when he thought that a composition wasn't any good: "put it deeply in the suitcase."[5]

Řídký soon took a special interest in Husa and was impressed with his pupil's rapid progress. Before long, he discussed with Husa's parents the possibility of enrolling Husa in the Prague Conservatory. When Řídký emphasized that Husa was more likely to be permitted to remain in Prague and away from the war zone, Husa's parents gave their permission. Husa began studying piano and conducting in addition to harmony and ear training, while continuing to compose whenever he could find the time. With the assistance of a tutor, Josef Blatný, Husa passed the entrance examinations to the Conservatory, and was admitted in 1941 to the the second year of a five-year program in composing and conducting.

Husa's conservatory years were largely spent studying composing with Řídký and conducting with Pavel Dědeček, attending what concerts the Nazis permitted (as well as some that they didn't), and continuing to help his father in the family shoe business. He continued to advance steadily, and in 1943 completed the first composition he deemed worthy of public performance, the *Sonatina*, for piano [W1]. He never regarded his second composition, a string quartet [W7], as more than a student work, and it never received a public performance. Another early work, *Overture*, for large orchestra [W27], was chosen for performance by the Czechoslovak Radio Orchestra in 1945. He requested and received permission to conduct this performance, and was gratified at the enthusiastic response of the orchestra to his conducting debut with a professional orchestra. He was invited to return, and conducted the orchestra several times in the following years.

Husa graduated from the Conservatory in 1945, immediately following the War, and entered a new graduate school, the Academy of Musical Arts, in the composition program. While still studying with Řídký, he completed the *Sinfonietta* [W28], the *Suite*, for viola and piano [W8], and the *Sonatina*, for violin and piano [W9]. He began to receive considerable public acclaim, both for his compositions and his conducting:

> By now, Husa's development was such that he was referred to as "one of the greatest hopes of Czech music."[6]

He also enjoyed many conducting performances at the Conservatory and the Academy, in addition to his broadcasts with the Czechoslovak Radio Orchestra.

During this time, Husa began to explore the possibility of going abroad to study. He hoped to travel for some years, and then return to Prague to complete his studies. With this in mind, he applied for three fellowships: one in Moscow, to study with Prokofiev; one in Paris to study with Honegger; and one in the United States. He placed his highest hopes on the French fellowship: "to study with Honegger was what I really wanted."[7] His mother also advised him to go to France for a year or two, and when in 1946, Husa heard Charles Munch conduct a performance in Prague, he knew that he wanted to study in Paris with

Honegger and Munch. After accepting a French government Fellowhip however, he was able to study only briefly with Munch, who left Paris shortly thereafter to become musical director of the Boston Symphony Orchestra. Husa continued his conducting studies with André Cluytens, the conductor of the Lyons Opera and conductor of the Société des Concerts at the Paris Conservatory.

Husa flourished during his studies with Arthur Honegger, and soon produced his longest work up to that time: *Three fresques* [W29a]. Like his previous compositions, this work was neoclassic in style.

> ... in the early works ... one finds carefully worked-out motives and phrase relationships, and neoclassical tonal implications. This concern for pitch detail and formal balance has stayed with Husa throughout his musical development and has been one of the reasons for his music's cohesiveness.[8]

In the summer of 1947, Husa returned to Prague and received a diploma from the Academy of Musical Arts that is regarded as equivalent to the Doctor of Musical Arts. At this time, the *Sinfonietta* [W28] received its premiere performance by the Czech Philharmonic, and Husa was invited to remain in Prague as assistant to Rafael Kubelík. He did not accept this offer, preferring to return to Paris, where his fellowship was renewed through 1948. Following his return, he was invited to meet Nadia Boulanger, who had become interested in Husa after examining his first composition, the *Sonatina*, for piano [W1]. Although he continued his formal studies with Honegger, he developed a close and lasting relationship with Boulanger. During this time, he completed requirements for the conducting and composition licenses at the École Normale de Musique. He also received his first commission, from the Smetana Quartet, which resulted in what eventually became his first *String quartet* [W10], and which won the Lili Boulanger Award in 1950, and the Bilthoven Festival Prize in 1952.

The French government Fellowship was due to expire in the spring of 1948, and with the rise of the Communist government in Czechoslovakia, Husa became concerned for his family still in Prague. In order to remain in Paris, he applied for a UNESCO Fellowship, an application that was warmly supported by Honegger. Although the Fellowship was administered by the United Nations, it required the approval of the Cultural Attaché in the Czechoslovakian Embassy in Paris. The Attaché questioned Husa, citing his lack of open support for the Communist government in Prague, and Husa withdrew his application.[9] Recognizing his success in Paris as a conductor and composer, however, the French government renewed his Fellowship for an additional five years.

Returning to Prague briefly in 1948, to conduct the Czechoslovak Radio Orchestra, Husa was again invited to remain and conduct, and again he declined.

> Being very young still, I didn't want to let anyone interfere with my plans, and thought I knew better than the Government. I am first a

composer, and then a conductor, mostly to support the composing. I hoped to follow the example of Bohuslav Martinů, who left Czechoslovakia and came to the U.S. at the start of World War II. I wanted to prove I was a composer, before I went back to live in Czechoslovakia.[10]

In 1949, Husa's passport expired, and he was advised by the Czechoslovakian government that he must return within one month or lose his citizenship. Reluctantly choosing not to return to his homeland, he forfeited his Czechoslovak citizenship and elected to remain in Paris as a refugee under the protection of the French Government.

My main reasons for not returning when ordered to were artistic, not only political. I would study for two to four years in Paris, go to the United States, travel, conduct and become a known composer. It was not mainly politics; I wanted to prove I'm a composer.[11]

When he failed to return in 1949, his properties, by Czech law, reverted to the State. Czech authorities went to his parents' home in Prague and confiscated his belongings there. They also attempted to take the piano, which did not belong to Husa, and did take the music which he had left behind. His father was encouraged to exert pressure on Husa, but he said: "Karel is 27 years old; how can I influence him? I don't expect he will come back."[12]

In Paris, he soon completed work on his conducting degree, and was awarded the Diploma in 1949 from the Conservatoire Nationale de Musique de Paris. The Director of the French Cultural Centre, Gilbert Gadoffre, invited Husa to move from his student dormitory at Cité Universitaire to Royaumont, an estate, formerly an Abbey, where artists could receive free room and board. Compositions from the period during which he lived at Royaumont include his *Concertino*, for piano and orchestra [W31a], *Sonata*, no.1, for piano [W2] and *Evocations de Slovaquie* [W11a].

In June of 1950, Husa was invited to go to the United States to assist Koussevitsky and teach conducting at Tanglewood; however, he had been ill during the previous winter, and had a recurrence in May. After a stay in the student hospital, followed by a period of recovery in a sanatorium outside Montblanc, he gave up his plans to go to America in the immediate future. It was during this time that he met his future wife Simone. They were married in 1952, and lived with her parents south of Paris, where he continued to compose, and received many invitations to appear as guest conductor with various orchestras. Works from this period include *Musique pour harmonie* [W53a] and *Musique d'amateurs* [W53b]. Husa also made some recordings during this time: Bartók's *Miraculous mandarin* and two *Rhapsodies*, for violin and orchestra, and, Brahms' first *Symphony*. He made several conducting appearances during the 1954 season, and was considered for the position of Music Director of the Symphony Orchestra of Monte Carlo. He applied for French citizenship at this time, planning to remain in France with his French wife and their young family.

Husa continued his composing activities, and finished several important works during the period that followed: the *Symphony*, no.1 [W32], the *String quartet*, no.2 [W12], and *Portrait*, for string orchestra [W33].

Husa had met Elliott Galkin in 1948 in Paris, where they had been classmates in conducting at the École Normale. Galkin left Paris in 1951, returning to the United States to study musicology at Cornell University. The two friends did not correspond, but Galkin immediately thought of Husa as a composer who could also conduct when, in 1954, the Chairman of the Music Department at Cornell, Donald Jay Grout, was searching for someone to replace a theory professor and later the orchestra conductor. Galkin wrote to Husa, as did Grout himself at a later date, explaining that the position was a three-year appointment, and asking Husa to apply immediately (March 1954) for the fall semester.

Husa felt there were many reasons to accept this position, and also thought it would be excellent for his composing. Nadia Boulanger and other admirers wrote letters strongly supporting Husa's candidacy, and he was soon hired. All of his records and transcripts had to be translated into English, and he did not really speak English at this time, having studied it for only a semester when he was 18. (In addition to Czech, he spoke German, had learned French from one of the veterans living in the apartment building in which he grew up, and had studied Russian during the War.) Husa and his family made plans to move to the United States, while Cornell officials worked with U.S. immigration officials to obtain a visa for him to enter the United States. On Sept. 28, 1954, Karel arrived in New York City; Simone followed with their two children two weeks later.

Husa was not able to spend much time composing during his first year in the United States. There were new classes to teach, requiring him to translate his knowledge into a language he had yet to master, and he would shortly assume various conducting duties as well. He did find the time, however, to write *Eight Czech duets* [W3] for his children, to help them learn some of the music of their heritage. He also wanted to make twentieth-century music more palatable to performers and amateur musicians, and with this intent, he composed *Four little pieces* [W34].

During 1955, while the director of the Cornell orchestras was on sabbatical leave, Husa served as interim director. The director returned in 1956, but left Cornell soon afterward, and in 1957, Husa became the director of the orchestras at Cornell, conducting six to seven concerts a year. The Cornell appointment was originally for only three years, but during his second year, Husa was offered a tenure-track position and he decided to stay in Ithaca, becoming an American citizen in 1959.

Compositions from this early Cornell period include the *Twelve Moravian songs* [W62], a work intended (like the *Eight Czech duets*) for young performers, and to keep alive folk songs of his native country. He also completed a commission, the *Fantasies*, for orchestra [W35], for the Friends of Music at Cornell.

Husa's mother died suddenly in the spring of 1957. His sister did not notify him until two weeks after the funeral, fearing that he would return to Prague, which would be dangerous for him. In memory of his mother, he composed *Elegie*, for piano [W4], intended as a tribute to the woman who had so inspired and influenced his musical education.

Continuing with his efforts to provide twentieth-century settings of Czech folk music, Husa arranged four of his *Eight Czech duets* [W3] in the composing of his *Divertimento*, for brass and percussion [W13a]. Composed in 1958, it received its premiere in 1960.

At the same time, Husa began moving away from tonality toward serialism. His first composition in this style, the *Poem*, for viola and chamber orchestra [W36], was premiered at the thirty-fourth World Music Festival of the International Society for Contemporary Music, held in Cologne during the summer of 1960. There it received much interested attention.[13]

Husa's French years had imbued him with a love of the saxophone, and when in 1959 Sigurd Rascher asked him to compose a piece for the saxophone, Husa transcribed his *Elegie* for piano [W4] for saxophone and piano, and added a new composition, resulting in his *Elegie et rondeau* [W14].

> The Elegie is somber and atonal, the Rondeau angry and flamboyant, with spectacular tour de force writing for the solo instrument.[14]

Early in 1961, Husa took a semester sabbatical and returned to Paris; while there he composed another serialistic work, *Mosaïques*, for orchestra [W38]. He also renewed his friendship with Nadia Boulanger, and conducted a memorial service for her mother and sister. In addition, with the support of a research grant from Cornell, he located three Baroque manuscripts in the Versailles Library and constructed modern performing editions of them [WA2, WA3, WA4]. He also conducted several performances while in Paris, and made a recording of his own *Fantasies*, for orchestra [D14].

Back in Ithaca in the summer of 1961, Husa prepared his Baroque editions for publication. In the next year, when he was asked to compose a work for the Baltimore Symphony Orchestra, for a woodwind quintet accompanied by orchestra, he decided to expand his *Evocations de Slovaquie* [W11a], resulting in the *Serenade*, for woodwind quintet with strings, harp and xylophone [W39]. He also reworked another composition during this period: the first movement of *Three fresques* [W29a] was rearranged and titled *Fresque*, for orchestra [W29b]. Its premiere took place in 1963, at a concert by the Syracuse University Orchestra.

Returning to the composition of instructional music, Husa composed *Festive ode* [W63] for the Centennial of Cornell University in 1964. During this time he was also asked to compose a work for brass quintet and chamber orchestra. The *Concerto*, for brass quintet and string orchestra [W40], originally intended for a

European tour by the New York Brass Quintet, was not premiered until 1970, when it was performed by the New England Conservatory Student Brass Quintet with the Buffalo Philharmonic.

Another commission from this period was the *Two preludes*, for flute, clarinet and bassoon [W15]. With this work, he began examining the outer ranges of the instruments, an experiment which continued with the composition of his *Concerto*, for saxophone and concert band [W54a].

> The soloist must have complete control of the entire 3 1/2 octave range of the instrument at all dynamic levels, and must be well versed in contemporary techniques. The ensemble needs to have strong players throughout who are equally capable of playing contemporary notation and techniques.[15]

In the fall of 1967, Husa was invited to give a seminar in composition at Ithaca College. At that time, Warren Benson, currently on that faculty, accepted an invitation to teach at the Eastman School of Music. As a result, Husa was offered a part-time position at Ithaca College, where he taught from 1967-1986. Also in the fall of 1967, he received a commission from the Fine Arts Quartet. Although planning an early 1968 trip to Europe to conduct, Husa was very anxious to fill this commission; he sketched out the quartet before his departure, and completed the full score immediately upon his return.[16] The *String quartet, no.3* [W16] had its premiere the following fall, and was very warmly received.

> It is a truly impressive achievement, the expression of one of the most interestingly human--and humane--musical minds in this country's recent history.[17]

The Fine Arts Quartet submitted the quartet to the selection committee for the Pulitzer Prize in music, and unaware that he had even been nominated, Husa was notified in the spring of 1969 that he was the winner of the 1969 Pulitzer Prize for music.

In 1968, Ithaca College commissioned a work for the College band. *Music for Prague, 1968* [W55] was premiered in 1969 at the Music Educators National Conference in Washington, D.C. Husa transcribed the work for orchestra during the following summer, and the orchestral version [W41] was premiered in Munich in early 1970. Together, both versions of the work have become standards in concert band and symphony orchestra repertoires, and have received over 7,000 performances.

> Although Erich Leinsdorf performed my *Mosaïques* in 1965, and the Fine Arts Quartet my third string quartet, it wasn't until 1968 and *Music for Prague* that publishers really started after me and my other music began to be played. For many of my published works, parts

were not available and had to be copied on the Library copier. Winning the Pulitzer Prize in 1969 created even more demand for my work to be performed.[18]

Husa returned to Prague in 1969, and at that time it was agreed that *Music for Prague, 1968* [W41] would be performed at the 1970 Prague Festival.

> In the fall of 1969, I was told they would still perform it, but with no date in the title. At Christmas, I was told that a shorter piece was required, so *Music for Prague* would be taken off the program, and *Mosaïques* substituted. In February, 1970, I was informed that Brezhnev would be visiting Prague on the day of the performance, so that only Soviet music would be performed, but that a concert later in the year would include my *Symphony* and *Serenade*.[19]

That concert never took place, although a recording of Husa's *Symphony* and *Serenade* was made by the Prague Symphony Orchestra, and issued by Composers Recordings, Inc. [D29]. Twenty years later, Husa was invited to return to Czechoslovakia and conduct *Music for Prague, 1968* for the first festival concert of the newly founded Association of Czech Musical Artists. The concert, which took place February 13, 1990, was a tribute to Civic Forum, the democracy movement led by Václav Havel.

The Michigan Band and Orchestra Association commissioned another band composition from Husa in 1970, and the result, *Apotheosis of this earth* [W56], was motivated by his concern for:

> . . . immense problems with everyday killings, war, hunger, extermination of fauna, huge forest fires and critical contamination of the whole environment. Man's brutal possession and misuse of nature's beauty--if continued at today's reckless speed--can only lead to catastrophe.[20]

Following a compositional trend evident in his music since the composition of his *Fantasies*, for orchestra, Husa's music has demonstrated an expanded role for percussion in large ensembles. This trend culminated in the composition of *Concerto*, for percussion and wind ensemble [W57], commissioned by the Ludwig Industries, and premiered in 1972.

After composing these three works for concert band, Husa returned to orchestral composition. *Two sonnets by Michelangelo* [W42] was commissioned by the Evanston (Illinois) Symphony Orchestra Association, and premiered in 1972. During this time, he was also working on what became his only composition for solo violin (discounting his early student works), the *Sonata*, for violin and piano [W17]. This sonata was a commission from the Koussevitsky Foundation, and received enthusiastic praise upon its premiere in 1974.

More commissions followed the *Sonata*. Husa composed the *Concerto*, for trumpet and wind orchestra [W58a] in response to a commission from two national honorary band fraternities. After completion of the *Concerto* in 1973, he was commissioned to write a memorial piece for the young son of a former student, killed in an automobile accident. *Steadfast tin soldier* [W43] follows the text of the Hans Christian Andersen fairy tale very closely, and at one point requires participation of children in the audience. Yet another commission, allowing him only a short time to complete the composition, resulted in *Al fresco*, for concert band [W59], a revision of *Fresque* [W29b].

> I always had some commission since 1967, and always just barely made deadlines. I would compose in the summer or Christmas breaks.[21]

During this period of hectic compositional activity, Husa continued to conduct, teach at both Cornell University and Ithaca College, and travel all over the United States and Europe.

> I was becoming more and more busy. I loved working with the student orchestras, it was part of my work, but was too time-consuming to compose. There was no assistant conductor at Cornell, and I was holding sectional and evening rehearsals, and managing the orchestras. Finally, in 1975 I decided it was all too much, turned the orchestras over to another professor and began teaching composition. Since then, I have had more free time (specifically in the evenings) to compose. It was hard work, but I loved every minute really seriously. It is more challenging, and I needed more time to compose. I wrote much more music since.[22]

Husa had not written a keyboard work since his *Elegie* [W4] in 1957, and in 1975, he began work on his *Sonata, no.2*, for piano [W5], a commission from the Edyth Bush Charitable Foundation. The *Sonata* was premiered by André-Michel Schub in 1975, and was later recorded, along with the *Sonatina* [W1], *Sonata, no.1* [W2] and the *Elegie* by Mary Ann Covert, an Ithaca College colleague of Husa's.

In 1975 the National Endowment for the Arts commissioned Husa's first ballet, for the Jordan College of Music at Butler University in Indianapolis. Inspired by James Baldwin's *The creative process*, *Monodrama* [W44] received its premiere in 1976, by the Butler Ballet and the Indianapolis Symphony Orchestra.

In 1976, Husa received a commission from Coe College in Cedar Rapids, Iowa, to commemorate the American Bicentennial and the 125th anniversary of the founding of the College. *An American Te Deum* [W65a], a long and intricate work, is scored for baritone solo, mixed chorus and wind ensemble.

An American Te Deum is the way I look at the U.S.: from an immigrant's point of view. Everybody wanted to work in this country.[23]

Two years later, Husa transcribed the original accompaniment of *An American Te Deum* for orchestra, and also conducted the East Coast premiere of the work.

During much of this time, Husa juxtaposed his teaching and composition with a demanding conducting schedule. Travelling all over the United States, and frequently to Europe and Asia, Husa worked extensively with young musicians.

I like to work as much with young people as with professional musicians. For the last six to eight years, I am asked so much to visit and conduct mostly with young people. When I was younger, each year in Europe, I conducted professional musicians; now, also young people, even high school. The challenge is going from the first rehearsal, when they hate you, to performance, when they understand.[24]

Performers are usually very good, and one has to challenge them. One has to go to the limits of possibilities, and this is how one learns. Every day I learn something that interests me.[25]

Never ceasing to write on commission, Husa composed *Landscapes*, for brass quintet [W18] in 1977, for the Western Brass Quintet of Kalamazoo, Michigan. The work was intended to be virtuosic and to reflect the sounds and moods of nature.

Three more commissions followed in 1979. *Three dance sketches*, for percussion quartet [W19] makes use of the different percussion families in three movements. *Pastoral*, for strings [W45] is an extensive revision of the slow movement of his *Sonatina*, for piano [W1]. A commission from the International Trumpet Guild completed Husa's output for this year, with *Intradas and interludes*, for 7 trumpets and percussion.

1980 was primarily given over to the composition of a major work, commissioned by the University of Louisville: a ballet to be performed by the Louisville Ballet and the University of Louisville Symphony Orchestra. Working with choreographer Alun Jones, Husa used a play by Euripides as the subject for the ballet. *The Trojan women* [W46a] was premiered in March, 1981, with several subsequent performances and a recording made in the same year. Speaking about the work, Husa says:

I want my music to move people, to alert them to this kind of tragedy. . . . I want them to realize that, even though 2,000 years have passed since the fall of Troy, we still have war and killing and no freedom."[26]

Husa received three more commissions in early 1981. A *Fanfare* [W21] was written to commemorate the twenty-fifth anniversary of the Portland (Oregon) Opera, and was premiered by the brass section of the Opera's orchestra prior to a performance of Wagner's *Die Walküre*. *Three Moravian songs* [W66], using three Moravian poems in an a cappella setting, was composed to fulfill a commission from the Holland (Michigan) Community Chorale. *Every day* [W67] was commissioned by the Ithaca College Concert Choir and is based on a text by Henry David Thoreau.

The next commission, from the Verdehr Trio, is scored for the unusual combination of violin, clarinet and piano. *Sonata a tre* [W22] features a single performer of the trio in each of the three movements. In a review of a concert by the Verdehr Trio, William Crutchfield calls the work a "standout,"

. . . with its sure sense of climax and dramatic variety in the instrumental handling.[27]

In 1982, while still working on the *Sonata a tre*, Husa began work on a new chamber work: *Recollections*, for woodwind quintet and piano [W23]. This work was one of four compositions commissioned by Grenadilla Records to commemorate 200 years of uninterrupted friendly relations between the United States and the Netherlands.

Another large-scale composition, a commission from Michigan State University, was the *Concerto*, for wind ensemble [W60], premiered in December of 1982. The *Concerto* features the technical skills not only of solo performers, but also of small groups within the larger ensemble. Husa's intent is for this work, like Stravinsky's *Symphonies of wind instruments*, to be performed by the wind sections of symphony orchestras as well as by symphonic bands.[28]

Other works completed during 1982-1983 include the *Cantata*, for men's chorus and brass quintet [W68], commissioned by the Wabash College Glee Club; *Symphony*, no.2 "Reflections" [W47], commissioned for the Eastern Music Festival in Greensboro, North Carolina; and a short work for winds, *Smetana fanfare* [W61], commissioned by the San Diego State University Wind Ensemble.

In 1984, Husa received three more commissions. *Variations*, for violin, viola, violoncello and piano [W24], composed on commission for the National Endowment for the Arts, was premiered in Atlanta by the Atlanta Virtuosi. In a review for *Musical America*, June Schneider quotes the composer's introductory remarks at the world premiere of the work:

. . . the quartet's sound-world refers constantly to bells, which operate musically and symbolically. They symbolize both unreality and real events: like the bells that rang in Prague in 1939, announcing defeat and the Nazi occupation; and the bells that sounded there again in 1945, ringing in victory and freedom. The bell motif also suggests church bells, a relentless reminder of the passage of time, denoting birth and death.[29]

Symphonic suite [W48] was commissioned by the University of Georgia to commemorate the bicentennial of its founding. *Intrada*, for brass quintet [W25] was composed for another commission by the National Endowment for the Arts for the Brass Menagerie.

It was just a life; one goes and the family grows. I can't believe it has been 34 years.[30]

Husa's most recent works have been large-scale orchestral compositions. The *Concerto*, for orchestra [W49] was commissioned by the New York Philharmonic, and premiered by that organization, conducted by Zubin Mehta, in 1985.

Cast in four continuous movements ("Cadence," "Fantasy," "In memoriam," and "Game"), with two connecting interludes, Husa's 38-minute *Concerto*, even more than Bartók's or Lutoslawski's, is filled with extraordinary challenges to instrumentalists and conductor.[31]

Two more concertos were written in 1987. The *Concerto*, for organ and orchestra [W50], was a commission from the Michelson-Morley Centennial Celebration. In this work, the virtuosic solo part is complemented by simpler writing for a reduced orchestra.

A practical composer, Husa likes to hear his music performed, and so he wrote his concerto to showcase the talents of a virtuoso organist while keeping the orchestral parts relatively simple. Like all of Husa's music, the concerto is crafted with assurance and expressed with honesty. A worthy addition to the limited repertoire for organ and orchestra. . . .[32]

The *Concerto*, for trumpet and orchestra [W51] was commissioned by Georg Solti and the Chicago Symphony Orchestra and premiered in 1988. Husa had the unique sound of the CSO's principal trumpet, Adolph Herseth, in mind when he conceived the work, and utilized classical orchestrations, although it includes no lower brass. Yet another concerto, the *Concerto*, for violoncello and orchestra

[W52] was commissioned by the University of Southern California and premiered in March of 1989. Husa describes the work in his own program notes:

> In the first part, *Introduction*, the cello solo begins in the lowest register in unison with all the cellos in the orchestra. . . . it detaches itself to become an independent voice and performs soloistically in the following *Recitative*. *Remembrance* is a slow, meditative movement. The last part is a *Hymn*, climaxing at the conclusion, in which the cello solo soars up to its highest register. . . .[33]

It should be evident that Husa shows no intention of slowing his compositional activity. In addition to his current work on a fourth string quartet [W26], commissioned by the National Endowment for the Arts for the Colorado String Quartet, and a violin concerto for Glenn Dicterow and the New York Philharmonic, Husa has expressed a desire to compose an opera. Although he is still looking for an acceptable libretto, it is not unlikely that he will begin work on an opera in the near future.

Known as an excellent technician, Husa nevertheless feels strongly that music should move and inspire its listeners.

> Music that is very well constructed has to have some sparks. I think that my older compositions show that I was still learning. I see this in practically all composers. The later works of all composers are architecturally the most powerful constructions. I like to be swept away in concerts.[34]

In May of 1989, Karel Husa received an award from the American Academy and Institute of Arts and Letters, to honor and encourage composers in their creative work. The award consisted of a monetary prize and included a compact disc recording to be made of one of his works, to be issued by Composers Recordings, Inc. The following citation was presented at the Academy's annual ceremony:

> Karel Husa is a composer of dramatic utterances, thoroughly of his time, his music breathes and seethes with emotional eloquence. But he goes beyond this and becomes a musical poet of imagination and power.[35]

NOTES

1. Donald Malcolm McLaurin, *The life and works of Karel Husa with emphasis on the significance of his contribution to the wind band.* (Ph.D. dissertation, Florida State University, 1985), 8.
2. Interview with Karel Husa, Ithaca, NY, Oct.3, 1987.
3. McLaurin, *Life and works of Karel Husa*, 10.
4. Interview with Husa, Ithaca, NY, Oct.3, 1987.
5. Ibid.
6. Lawrence W. Hartzell, "Karel Husa: the man and the music." *Musical quarterly* 62, no.1 (January 1976): 88.
7. Interview with Husa, Ithaca, NY, Oct.3, 1987.
8. Hartzell, "Karel Husa", 93.
9. McLaurin, *Life and works of Karel Husa*, 31.
10. Interview with Husa, Ithaca, NY, Oct.3, 1987.
11. Ibid.
12. Ibid.
13. Willi Schuh, "Das 34. Weltmusikfest in Köln." *Schweizerische Musikzeitung* 100, no.5: 134.
14. Robert T. Jones, "Classics at core of Czech concert, *New York Times*, April 29, 1969, p.40.
15. Paul Cohen, "Vintage saxophones revisited: 'classic' band music for the saxophone soloist." *Saxophone journal*, March/April, 1989: 8-10.
16. McLaurin, *Life and works of Karel Husa*, 62.
17. Elliott W. Galkin, "A deserving music Pulitzer winner," *Baltimore Sun*, May 11, 1969.
18. Interview with Husa, Ithaca, NY, Oct.3, 1987.
19. Ibid.
20. David Ewen, "Karel Husa, 1921-" *Composers since 1900*, first supplement. (New York: H.W. Wilson, 1981), 157.
21. Interview with Husa, Ithaca, NY, Oct.3, 1987.
22. Ibid.
23. Ibid.
24. Ibid.
25. Ibid.
26. George Sturm, "Husa's *Trojan women* triumphs in Louisville," *MadAminA!* 2, no.2 (Fall 1981): 4.
27. William Crutchfield, "Verdehr Trio promotes a rare configuration." *New York Times*, March 5, 1989, sect.1, p.67.
28. Letter from the composer, March 9, 1989.
29. June Schneider, "Atlanta Virtuosi: piano quartets by Husa, Schuller, Schwartz [premieres]." *High fidelity/Musical America* 34 (November, 1984): MA24.
30. Interview with Husa, Ithaca, NY, Oct.3, 1987.
31. Elliott W. Galkin, "New York Philharmonic: Husa 'Concerto for orchestra.'" *Musical America* 107, no.1 (March 1987): 27.
32. Wilma Salisbury, "Creativity warmly received," *Cleveland Plain Dealer*, Oct.30, 1987, p.11.

33.   Karel Husa, "Concerto for violoncello and orchestra (1988)."
      Program, University of Southern California Symphony, March 2,
      1989.
34.   Interview with Husa, Ithaca, NY, Oct.3, 1987.
35.   Citation from the American Academy and Institute of Arts and Letters,
      May 17, 1989.

Works and Performances

The compositions listed are organized by genre and subarranged chronologically by date of composition. The "SEE" references identify citations in the "Bibliography" and "Discography" sections, e.g. B546, and D17. The instrumentation of a given work follows the usual pattern: woodwinds, brasses, timpani, percussion and strings. Piano reductions of works for solo instrument with large ensemble are listed separately only if they received what the composer regards as a significant premiere performance. Most works that are revisions, expansions and/or arrangements of a work for another performance medium are listed with the original composition; however, if a subsequent version of a work has become a standard in another perfomance repertoire, it is numbered separately and listed under the appropriate genre. Except where noted, all manuscripts are in the possession of the composer. Photocopies of all manuscripts are owned by Ithaca College, Ithaca, New York.

WORKS FOR KEYBOARD

W1. *Sonatina* (1943) (12 min.)
> For piano
> Premiere: 20 April, 1945, Prague, Czechoslovakia
> Performer: Jiří Berkovec
> Prague: Fr. Urbanek, 1947 [dist. by Boosey & Hawkes]
> New York: Associated Music Publishers, 1947 [a new engraving of the Urbanek ed.]
> SEE: B36, B138, B322, B424; D24

W2. *Sonata,* no. 1 (1949) (ca. 26 min.)
> For piano
> Premiere: 19 April, 1950, Paris, France

Performer: Luise Vosgerchian
Mainz: Schott, 1952
SEE: B90, B138, B424, B456, B465; D24

W3.   *Eight Czech duets* (1955) (20 min.)
For piano (4 hands)
Premiere: 28 April, 1956, Cornell University Festival of Contemporary
Arts, Ithaca, New York
Performer: Bruce Archibald and Charles McClain
Mainz: Schott, 1958
SEE: B424; D10

W4.   *Elegie* (1957) (5 min.)
For piano
Premiere: 15 November, 1967, Ithaca College, Ithaca, New York
Performer: Elaine Merrey
Paris: Leduc, 1968
SEE: B138, B424; D24

W5.   *Sonata,* no. 2 (1975) (18 min.)
For piano
Commissioned by the Edyth Bush Charitable Foundation for the
Bicentennial Piano Series of the Washington Performing Arts Society
Premiere: 4 October, 1975, Washington, D.C.
Performer: André-Michel Schub
New York: Associated Music Publishers, 1978
SEE: B35-B36, B67, B70, B138, B146, B299, B322, B367, B419, B547;
D24-D25

W6.   *Frammenti* (1987) (6 min.)
For organ
Excerpts for solo organ, from the *Concerto,* for organ and orchestra; see
W50
Premiere: 6 November, 1987, Northwestern University, Evanston,
Illinois
Performer: Karel Paukert, organ
New York : Associated Music Publishers, [NYP]
SEE: B521, B528, B543

WORKS FOR CHAMBER ENSEMBLE

W7.   *String quartet* (1943) (ca. 20 min.)
Premiere: private performance in Prague, Czechoslovakia, March 1944
Performer: Prague Quartet
Unpublished

W8. *Suite* (1945) (ca. 15 min.)
For viola and piano
Premiere: 26 November, 1946, Prague, Czechoslovakia
Performer: Antonin Hyksa, viola; Jiří Berkovec, piano
Unpublished

W9. *Sonatina* (1945) (ca. 15 min.)
For violin and piano
Premiere: 27 September, 1945, Prague, Czechoslovakia
Performer: Spytihněv Šorm, violin; Otakar Pařík, piano
Unpublished
The manuscript is held privately in Prague, Czechoslovakia

W10. *String quartet*, no. 1 (1948) (24 min.)
Commissioned by the Smetana Quartet
Premiere: 23 May, 1948, Prague, Czechoslovakia
Performer: Smetana Quartet
Mainz: Schott, 1948
Lili Boulanger Foundation Prize, 1950; Bilthoven (Gaudeamus) Festival
Prize, 1952
[Initially titled *String quartet no.2*, Husa renumbered this work, as W7
was never performed publicly]
SEE: B159, B296, B349; D27

W11a. *Evocations de Slovaquie* (1951) (15 min.)
For clarinet, viola and violoncello
Premiere: 4 May, 1952, Paris, France
Performer: Maurice Cliquenois, clarinet; Micheline Lemoine, viola;
Jacques Neiltz, violoncello
Mainz: Schott, 1970
SEE: B126, B139, B176, B367, B460; D13

W11b. *Evocations de Slovaquie* (1988) (15 min.)
For flute, viola and violoncello
Premiere: 8 April, 1988, New York City, New York
Performer: Robert Stallman, flute; Members of the Muir quartet
Unpublished

W12. *String quartet*, no. 2 (1953) (20 min.)
Commissioned by the Parrenin String Quartet of Paris
Premiere: 23 October, 1954, Paris, France
Performer: Parrenin String Quartet
Mainz: Schott, 1953
SEE: B59, B159, B169, B171, B296, B343, B349, B434, B509, B526, B527;
D28

W13a. *Divertimento* (1958) (15 min.)
For brass ensemble and percussion
Expansion of movements from *Eight Czech duets*; see W3
Premiere: 17 February, 1960, Ithaca, New York

Performer: Ithaca College Brass Ensemble; conducted by Robert Prins
New York: Associated Music Publishers, 1970
SEE: B77, B108, B115, B250, B339, B346, B349

W13b. *Divertimento* (1968) (16 min.)
For brass quintet
Expansion of movements from *Eight Czech duets*; see W3
Premiere: 20 November, 1968, Ithaca College, Ithaca, New York
Performer: Ithaca Brass Quintet
New York: Associated Music Publishers, 1968
SEE: B144, B291; D8-D9

W14. *Elegie et rondeau* (1960) (10 min.)
For alto saxophone and piano
Elegie from W4; *Rondeau* is a new composition
Premiere: July 29, 1960, at the Eastman School of Music Summer
Saxophone Symposium, Rochester, New York
Performer: Sigurd Rascher, saxophone; William Krevis, piano
Paris: Leduc, 1961
SEE: B177, B253, B313, B339, B349; D11-D12

W15. *Two preludes* (1966) (12 min.)
For flute, clarinet and bassoon
Commissioned by the Iota (Ithaca College) chapter of Kappa Kappa Psi
(national music fraternity)
Premiere: 22 April, 1966, Ithaca College, Ithaca, New York
Performer: William Hoff, flute; Joseph Amisano, clarinet; Donald
Winch, bassoon
Paris: Leduc, 1968
SEE: B346, B400, B454; D32

W16. *String quartet*, no. 3 (1968) (19 min.)
Commissioned by the Fine Arts Foundation of Chicago
Premiere: 14 October, 1968, Chicago, Illinois
Performer: Fine Arts String Quartet
New York: Associated Music Publishers, 1970
Pulitzer Prize for Music, 1969
SEE: B99, B102, B123, B148, B152-B153, B159, B168, B178-B179,
B184-B185, B191, B199-B201, B247, B249, B254, B272, B290-B292, B296,
B298, B314, B323, B325, B349, B369-B370, B373, B389, B403, B410,
B428, B433-B434, B486, B518, B528, B542; D28

W17. *Sonata* (1973) (30 min.)
For violin and piano
Commissioned by the Koussevitzky Foundation
Premiere: 30 March, 1974, New York City, New York
Performer: Ani Kavafian, violin; Richard Goode, piano
New York: Associated Music Publishers, 1979
SEE: B90, B104, B122, B163, B297, B346, B354, B371-B372, B416, B484,
B499, B545; D26

W18. *Landscapes* (1977) (22 min.)
For brass quintet
Commissioned by the Western Brass Quintet for the Bicentennial of the
United States
Premiere: 17 October, 1977, Kalamazoo, Michigan
Performer: Western Brass Quintet
New York: Associated Music Publishers, 1978
SEE: B142, B144, B301, B339, B422; D17

W19. *Three dance sketches* (1979) (18 min.)
For four percussionists
Commissioned by the National Association of College Wind and
Percussion Instructors
Premiere: 12 April, 1980, at the 27th National Music Educators National
Conference biennial Convention, Miami, Florida
Performer: University of Tennessee Percussion Ensemble; conducted by
H. Michael Comb
New York: Associated Music Publishers, 1982
SEE: B11, B234, B423, B514

W20. *Intradas and interludes* (1980) (17 min.)
For 7 trumpets and percussion
Commissioned by the International Trumpet Guild
Premiere: 21 June, 1980, at Ohio State University, for the International
Trumpet Guild annual convention, Columbus, Ohio
Performer: International Trumpet Guild Ensemble; conducted by
Marshall Haddock
New York: Associated Music Publishers, 1985
SEE: B263, B423

W21. *Fanfare* (1981) (6 min.)
For brass ensemble and percussion
Commissioned by the Portland (Oregon) Opera
Premiere: 7 March, 1981, Portland, Oregon
Performer: Portland Opera Brass ensemble; conducted by Fred Sautter
New York: Associated Music Publishers, 1984

W22. *Sonata a tre* (1981) (20 min.)
For violin, clarinet and piano
Commissioned by the Verdehr Trio
Premiere: 23 March, 1982, Hong Kong
Performer: Verdehr Trio
New York: Associated Music Publishers, 1987
SEE: B112, B382, B477, B511, B514-B515, B531; D23

W23. *Recollections* (1982) (21 min.)
For woodwind quintet and piano
Commissioned by the Grenadilla Enterprises to celebrate the
bicentennial of Dutch-American diplomatic relations
Premiere: 28 October, 1982, The Library of Congress, Washington, D.C.

Performer: New Amsterdam Ensemble; Walter Ponce, piano
New York: Associated Music Publishers, [NYP]
SEE: B110, B276, B334, B379, B397, B451, B511, B514

W24.   *Variations* (1984) (21 min.)
For violin, viola, violoncello and piano
Commissioned by the National Endowment for the Arts for the
   consortium of the Atlanta Virtuosi, the Rowe Quartet and the New
   England Piano Quartette
Premiere: 20 May, 1984, Atlanta, Georgia
Performer: Atlanta Virtuosi
New York: Associated Music Publishers, [NYP]
SEE: B164, B208-B209, B262, B320, B474-B475, B518, 520; D34

W25.   *Intrada* (1984) (3 min.)
For brass quintet
Commissioned by the Brass Menagerie and the National Endowment
   for the Arts
Premiere: 15 November, 1984, Festival of the Arts, Baltimore, Maryland
Performer: The Brass Menagerie
Unpublished

W26.   *String quartet*, no. 4 (in progress)
Commissioned by the National Endowment for the Arts for the
   Colorado Quartet
SEE: B515

SEE ALSO W65d

WORKS FOR ORCHESTRA

W27.   *Overture* (1944) (ca. 8 min.)
For orchestra (3-3-3-3; 4-3-3-1; timp; 3 perc; hp; str)
Premiere: 20 January, 1945, Prague, Czechoslovakia (broadcast); 18
   June, 1946, Prague, Czechoslovakia (concert)
Performer: Czechoslovak Radio Orchestra (broadcast); Prague
   Symphony Orchestra (concert); both performances conducted by the
   composer
Unpublished

W28.   *Sinfonietta* (1944) (ca. 20 min.)
For orchestra (3-2-2-2; 2-2-0-0; timp; 3 perc; hp; str)
Premiere: 25 April, 1947, Prague, Czechoslovakia
Performer: Czechoslovak Radio Orchestra; conducted by Karel Ancerl
Prague: Czech Musical Fund, [n.d.]
Awarded Prague Academy of Arts and Sciences Prize, 1948

W29a. *Three fresques* (1947) (ca. 27 min.)
For orchestra (3-3-3-3; 4-3-3-1; timp; 3 perc; hp; pno; str)
Premiere: 27 April, 1949, Prague, Czechoslovakia
Performer: Prague Radio Orchestra; conducted by Václav Smetáček
Prague: Czech Musical Fund, [n.d.]

W29b. *Fresque* (1963) (11 min.)
For orchestra (3-3-3-3; 4-3-3-1; 3 perc; hp; pno; str)
Revision of first movement of *Three fresques*; see W29a
Premiere: 5 May, 1963, Syracuse, New York
Performer: Syracuse University Orchestra; conducted by the composer
New York: Associated Music Publishers, 1976
SEE: B20, B457

W30. *Divertimento* (1948) (15 min.)
For string orchestra
Premiere: 30 October, 1949, Paris, France
Performer: Club d'essai Paris Orchestra; conducted by Stanislaw
Skrowacewski
Mainz: Schott, 1977
SEE: B459

W31a. *Concertino* (1949) (15 min.)
For piano and orchestra (2-2-2-2; 2-2-0-0; perc; str)
Premiere: 6 June, 1952, Brussels, Belgium
Performer: Helene Boschi, piano; Belgian Radio and Television
Orchestra; conducted by Daniel Sternfeld
Mainz: Schott, [n.d.]

W31b. *Concertino* [revised version] (1983) (16 min.)
For piano and wind ensemble
Commissioned by the University of Central Florida Department of
Music, Jerry Gardner, director
Premiere: 27 January, 1984, at the combined meetings of the College
Band Directors National Association and the National Band
Association, Southern Divisions, Orlando, Florida
Performer: Gary Wolf, piano; University of Central Florida Wind
Ensemble; conducted by the composer
Unpublished
SEE: B525

W32. *Symphony*, no. 1 (1953) (27 min.)
For orchestra (3-3-3-2; 4-3-3-1; perc; hp (2); pno; str)
Premiere: 4 March, 1954, Brussels, Belgium
Performer: Belgian Radio and Television Orchestra; conducted by
Daniel Sternfeld
Mainz: Schott, 1953
SEE: B20, B40, B62-B63, B98, B172-B173, B248, B269, B368, B399, B436,
B452, B467, B490, B503, B540, B563-B564; D29

W33.   *Portrait*   (1953)   (12 min.)
For string orchestra
Commissioned by the Donaueschingen Musiktage
Premiere: 10 October, 1953, Donaueschingen, W. Germany
Performer: Süd-Westfunk Radio Orchestra; conducted by Hans Rosbaud
Mainz: Schott, 1977
SEE: B78, B501, B508, B523

W34.   *Four little pieces*   (1955)   (16 min.)
For strings (orchestra or soloists)
Premiere: 17 March, 1957, at the Youth Music Festival, Fürsteneck Castle, West Germany
Performer: Ensemble of the Youth Music Festival, conducted by Hilmar Hockner
Mainz: Schott, 1955
SEE: B76, B131, B337, B348; D16

W35.   *Fantasies*   (1956)   (19 min.)
For orchestra   (1 (pic)-1-1-0;0-3-0-0; perc; pno; str)
Commissioned by the Friends of Music at Cornell University
Premiere: 28 April, 1957, Cornell University Festival of Contemporary Arts, Ithaca, New York
Performer: Cornell University Orchestra; conducted by the composer
Mainz: Schott, 1961
SEE: B15, B114, B118, B127, B161, B189, B283, B368; D14-D15, D29

W36.   *Poem*   (1959)   (13 min.)
For viola and chamber orchestra   (ob, hn, pno, str)
Premiere: 12 June, 1960, World Music Festival of the International Society for Contemporary Music, Cologne, West Germany
Performer: Ulrich Koch, viola; Süd-Westfunk Radio Orchestra; conducted by Hans Rosbaud
Mainz: Schott, 1963
Also available for viola and piano
SEE: B101, B166, B261, B306, B376, B430, B476, B492

W37.   *Elegie et rondeau*   (1961)   (10 min.)
For alto saxophone and orchestra   (2-2-2-2; 2-2-0-0; perc; pno; str)
Originally for saxophone and piano; see W14
Premiere: 6 May, 1962, Cornell University Festival of Contemporary Arts, Ithaca, New York
Performer: Sigurd Rascher, saxophone; Cornell Symphony Orchestra; conducted by the composer
Paris: Leduc, [n.d.]
SEE: B287

W38.   *Mosaïques*   (1961)   (15 min.)
For orchestra   (1 (pic)-1 (E.hn)-1 (bcl)-1; 2-2-2-0; timp; perc; cel; hp; str)
Commissioned by the Hamburg Radio Corporation

Premiere: 7 November, 1961, Hamburg, W. Germany
Performer: Nord-Deutscher Rundfunk Orchester; conducted by the
composer
Mainz: Schott, 1977
SEE: B48, B58, B109, B135, B356, B401, B438, B491, B504, B551; D18

W39. *Serenade* (1963) (15 min.)
For woodwind quintet, strings, harp and xylophone
Expansion of *Evocations de Slovaquie*; see W11a
Commissioned by the Baltimore Symphony Orchestra
Premiere: 7 January, 1964, Baltimore, Maryland
Performer: Baltimore Symphony Orchestra; conducted by Peter
Herman Adler
Paris: Leduc, 1965
Also available for woodwind quintet and piano
SEE: B63, B77, B96, B98, B116, B169, B198, B207, B221, B258, B306, B333,
B339, B348, B368, B376, B430, B437, B564; D29

W40. *Concerto* (1965) (24 min.)
For brass quintet and string orchestra
Premiere: 15 February, 1970, Buffalo, New York
Performer: New England Conservatory Student Brass Quintet; Buffalo
Philharmonic Orchestra; conducted by Lukas Foss
Paris: Leduc, 1971
Also available for brass quintet and piano
SEE: B42, B134, B224, B405, B411, B435, B536

W41. *Music for Prague, 1968* (1969) (19 min.)
For orchestra (3-3-3-3; 4-4-3-1; timp; 4 perc; hp; pno; str)
Originally for concert band; see W55
Premiere: 31 January, 1970, Munich, West Germany
Performer: Munich Philharmonic Orchestra; conducted by the
composer
New York: Associated Music Publishers, 1969
SEE: B28, B46, B54-B56, B71, B80, B91-B92, B103, B113, B115-B116, B121,
B131-B133, B136, B145, B160, B167, B180, B196-B198, B201, B211-B212,
B217, B219, B227, B231, B241, B244, B247, B284, B289, B293-B295,
B297-B298, B303, B305, B307, B323, B341, B383-B385, B394, B406,
B408, B439-B440, B442, B449, B461-B464, B471, B482, B502, B506,
B510, B515, B533, B535, B537, B550, B556, B560, B563, B566-B568; D22

W42. *Two sonnets by Michelangelo* (1971) (16 min.)
For orchestra (3-3-3-2; 4-3-3-1; timp; perc; hp; str)
Commissioned by the Evanston (Illinois) Symphony Orchestra
Association
Premiere: 28 April, 1972, Evanston, Illinois
Performer: Evanston Symphony Orchestra; conducted by Frank Miller
New York: Associated Music Publishers, 1975
SEE: B71, B119, B155, B177, B182, B223, B412, B457; D33

W43.   *The steadfast tin soldier* (1974) (26 min.)
For narrator and orchestra (2-2-2-2; 2-2-0-0; timp; hp; perc; str)
Commissioned by the John Ernest Fowler Memorial Fund
Text from the Hans Christian Andersen fairy tale
Premiere: 10 May, 1975, Boulder, Colorado
Performer: John Paton, narrator; Boulder Philharmonic Orchestra
conducted by the composer
New York: Associated Music Publishers, 1974
SEE: B182, B298, B330, B418

W44.   *Monodrama: portrait of an artist,* ballet (1976) (23 min.)
For orchestra (3-3-3-3; 4-3-3-1; timp; perc; hp; str)
Commissioned by the National Endowment for the Arts for the Jordan
College of Music of Butler University and the Bicentennial of the
United States
Premiere: 26 March, 1976, Indianapolis, Indiana
Performer: The Butler Ballet; the Indianapolis Symphony Orchestra;
conducted by Oleg Kovalenko
New York: Associated Music Publishers, 1979
SEE: B35, B67, B181, B192, B299, B322, B413, B420

W45.   *Pastoral* (1979) (7 min.)
For string orchestra
Derived from the 2nd movement of the *Sonatina,* for piano; see W1
Commissioned by the American String Teachers Association
Premiere: 12 April, 1980, at the 27th Music Educators National
Conference biennial Convention, Miami, Florida
Performer: ASTA National String Orchestra
New York: Associated Music Publishers, 1982
SEE: B337, B414, B423, B514

W46a.   *The Trojan women,* ballet (1980) (45 min.)
For orchestra (2-2-2-2; 2-2-1-0; timp; 3 perc; hp; pno; str)
Commissioned by the University of Louisville School of Music
Premiere: 28 March, 1981, Louisville, Kentucky
Performer: Louisville Ballet; University of Louisville Orchestra;
conducted by the composer
New York: Associated Music Publishers, 1981
SEE: B41, B51, B174, B204, B232, B350, B352-B353, B478, B513, B520,
B552, B562, B565; D30

W46b.   *The Trojan women,* suite (1984) (22 min.)
For orchestra (2-2-2-2; 2-2-1-0; timp; 3 perc; hp; pno; str)
Premiere: 28 October, 1988, Metropolitan Museum of Art, New York
City, New York
Performer: Orchestra of St. Luke's; conducted by the composer
New York: Associated Music Publishers, [NYP]
SEE: B83, B111, B275

W47. *Symphony*, no. 2 "Reflections" (1983) (20 min.)
For orchestra (2-2-2-2; 2-2-0-0; timp; perc; hp; str)
Commissioned for the Eastern Music Festival
Premiere: 16 July, 1983, Greensboro, North Carolina
Performer: Eastern Philharmonic Orchestra; conducted by the composer
New York: Associated Music Publishers, 1983
SEE: B206, B245, B319, B360, B511, B530

W48. *Symphonic suite* (1984) (19 min.)
For orchestra (3-3-3-3; 4-3-3-1; timp; 4 perc; hp; pno; str)
Commissioned by the University of Georgia for the bicentennial celebration of its charter
Premiere: 1 October, 1984, Athens, Georgia
Performer: University of Georgia Festival Orchestra; conducted by the composer
New York: Associated Music Publishers, 1984
The manuscript is owned by the University of Georgia and housed in the University Libraries, Athens, Georgia
SEE: B381, B473, B518, B520

W49. *Concerto* (1986) (39 min.)
For orchestra (3-3-3-3; 4-3-3-1; timp; 4 perc; hp; pno; str)
Commissioned by the New York Philharmonic and Zubin Mehta
Premiere: 25 September, 1986, New York City, New York
Performer: The New York Philharmonic; conducted by Zubin Mehta
New York: Associated Music Publishers, [NYP]
SEE: B28, B37-B38, B47, B52, B86-B87, B160, B170, B188, B220, B238, B260, B278, B375, B441, B569

W50. *Concerto* (1987) (21 min.)
For organ and orchestra (3 tpts; timp; 2 perc; str)
Commissioned by the Michelson-Morley Centennial Celebration, 1987
Premiere: 28 October, 1987, Cleveland Museum of Art, Cleveland, Ohio
Performer: Karel Paukert, organ; The Cleveland Institute of Music Orchestra; conducted by the composer
New York : Associated Music Publishers, [NYP]
SEE: B88, B158, B165, B453, B468, B519

W51. *Concerto* (1987) (20 min.)
For trumpet and orchestra (2-2-2-2; 2-2-0-0; timp; 3 perc; hp; str)
Commissioned by the Chicago Symphony Orchestra
Premiere: 11 February, 1988, Chicago, Illinois
Performer: Adolph Herseth, trumpet; The Chicago Symphony Orchestra; conducted by Sir Georg Solti
New York: Associated Music Publishers, [NYP]
SEE: B39, B85, B95, B105-B106, B165, B202, B240, B273, B326-B328, B355, B392, B519, B548-B549, B561

W52.   *Concerto* (1988) (28 min.)
For violoncello and orchestra (3-3-3-3; 4-3-3-1; timp; 3 perc; hp; str)
Commissioned by the University of Southern California, for the Frank
  Kerze Jr. Memorial Fund
Premiere: 2 March, 1989
Performer: Lynn Harrell, violoncello; The University of Southern
  California Symphony; conducted by Daniel Lewis
Unpublished
The commission and world premiere performance is dedicated, in
  memorial, to Frank Kerze Jr. by his sisters Terese Kerze Cheyovich
  and Florence Kerze.
SEE: B4, B81, B90, B165, B274, B336, B444, B458, B512, B515

SEE ALSO W53b

SEE ALSO W60

WORKS FOR BAND

W53a. *Musique pour harmonie* (1951) (ca. 15 min.)
For winds and percussion
Commissioned by UNESCO
No known public performance
Unpublished

W53b. *Musique d'amateurs* (1953) (15 min.)
For orchestra (ob, tpt, perc, str)
Commissioned by UNESCO
Premiere: 1954, Castle Frubeck, W. Germany
Performer: U.N.E.S.C.O. chamber orchestra; conducted by Hilmar
  Hockner
Mainz: Schott, 1977

W54a. *Concerto* (1967) (20 min.)
For alto saxophone and concert band
Commissioned by the Cornell University Wind Ensemble, Maurice
  Stith, director
Premiere: 17 March, 1968, Ithaca, New York
Performer: Sigurd Rascher, saxophone; Cornell University Wind
  Ensemble; conducted by the composer
New York: Associated Music Publishers, 1972
SEE: B15, B18, B77, B93, B120, B177, B291, B293, B321, B323-B324, B393,
  B402, B409, B483, B546; D1, D4-D5

W54b. *Concerto* (1972) (20 min.)
For alto saxophone and piano
Premiere: 1972, Evanston, Illinois

Performer: Fred Hemke, saxophone; Milton Granger, piano
New York: Associated Music Publishers, 1972
SEE: D6-D7

W55. *Music for Prague, 1968* (1968) (19 min.)
For concert band
See also version for orchestra: W41
Commissioned by Ithaca College Band, Kenneth Snapp, director
Premiere: 31 January, 1969, at the national convention of the Music
Educators National Conference, Washington, D.C.
Performer: Ithaca College Concert Band; conducted by Kenneth Snapp
New York: Associated Music Publishers, 1969
SEE: B7, B12-B13, B24, B30, B33, B45, B175, B196, B201, B246, B250,
B274, B277, B281, B292, B295, B297-B298, B404, B448, B483, B498,
B539, B555; D3, D5, D19-D21

W56. *Apotheosis of this earth* (1970) (25 min.)
For concert band
See also version for chorus and orchestra: W64
Commissioned by the Michigan Band and Orchestra Association, and
dedicated to William D. Revelli on the occasion of his retirement
Premiere: 1 April, 1971, Ann Arbor, Michigan
Performer: University of Michigan Symphonic Band; conducted by the
composer
New York: Associated Music Publishers, 1971
SEE: B2-B3, B17, B24-B26, B30, B33, B53, B71, B150, B154, B175, B195,
B295, B297, B308, B318, B321, B338, B359, B364, B380, B407, B541,
B557; D3

W57. *Concerto* (1971) (18 min.)
For percussion and wind ensemble
Commissioned by Ludwig Industries
Premiere: 7 February, 1972, Waco, Texas
Performer: Baylor University Symphonic Wind Ensemble; conducted
by Gene C. Smith and Larry Vanlandingham
New York: Associated Music Publishers, 1973
SEE: B14-B15, B156, B223, B282, B386, B415, B427, B429, B448, B539,
B546, B553, B557; D1

W58a. *Concerto* (1973) (14 min.)
For trumpet and wind orchestra (3-3-3-3; 4-3-3-1; timp.; 4 perc; str.b.)
Commissioned by Kappa Kappa Psi and Tau Beta Sigma (national
honorary band fraternities)
Premiere: 9 August, 1973, at the biennial convention of Kappa Kappa
Psi and Tau Beta Sigma, University of Connecticut, Storrs,
Connecticut
Performer: Raymond Crisara, trumpet, National Intercollegiate Band;
conducted by Arnold Gabriel
New York: Associated Music Publishers, 1980
SEE: B22, B104, B117, B157, B280, B514, B557

W58b. *Concerto* (1976) (14 min.)
    For trumpet and piano
    Premiere: 13 November, 1977, Cornell University, Ithaca, New York
    Performer: Maurice Stith, trumpet; Brian Israel, piano
    New York: Associated Music Publishers, 1982

W59. *Al fresco* (1974) (12 min.)
    For band
    Derived from the first movement of *Three fresques*; see W29a
    Commissioned by Ithaca College
    Premiere: 19 April, 1975, Ithaca College, Ithaca, New York
    Performer: Ithaca College Concert Band; conducted by the composer
    New York: Associated Music Publishers, 1975
    SEE: B16, B30, B50, B77, B119, B203, B246, B417, B546, D1-D2

W60. *Concerto* (1982) (19 min.)
    For wind ensemble
    Commissioned by Michigan State University Alumni Band, for the
        opening of the Wharton Center for the Performing Arts
    Premiere: 3 December, 1982, East Lansing, Michigan
    Performer: Michigan State University Wind Symphony; conducted by
        the composer
    New York: Associated Music Publishers, 1982
    Winning composition in the first biennial Sudler International Wind
        Band Composition Competition
    The composer notes that this work can also be performed by the wind
        sections of symphony orchestras.
    SEE: B89, B186-B187, B222, B262, B268, B271, B347, B378, B395, B450,
        B511, B518, B525

W61. *Smetana fanfare* (1984) (4 min.)
    For band
    Commissioned by San Diego State University Wind Ensemble; Charles
        Yates, director
    Premiere: 3 April, 1984, San Diego, California, commemorating the
        100th anniversary of Smetana's death
    Performer: San Diego State University Wind Ensemble; conducted by
        Charles Yates
    New York: Associated Music Publishers, 1989
    SEE: B89, B175, B246, B274, B318, B515

SEE ALSO W31b

WORKS FOR SOLO VOICE OR CHORUS

W62. *Twelve Moravian songs* (1956) (27 min.)
For voice and piano
Text from folk texts
Premiere: April 1968, Brno, Czechoslovakia
Performer: Unknown singer and pianist for the Czechoslovak Radio-Television of Brno
New York: Associated Music Publishers, 1977
SEE: B31; D31

W63. *Festive ode* (1964) (4 min.)
For mixed chorus and orchestra (3-3-3-3; 4-4-3-1; timp; perc; hp; pno; str)
Text by Eric Blackall
Premiere: 9 October, 1964, Cornell University Centennial Convocation, Ithaca, New York
Performer: Cornell University Symphony Orchestra, Chorus and Glee Club; conducted by Thomas A. Sokol
New York: Highgate Press, 1977
Also available in version for mixed chorus and band or brass ensemble, or organ
SEE: B71

W64. *Apotheosis of this earth* (1972) (25 min.)
For mixed chorus and orchestra (4-4-4-4; 4-4-4-1; timp; perc; str; opt. 2 al sax, ten sax, bar sax)
A new version of W56
Text by the composer
Premiere: 12 April, 1973, Cornell University, Ithaca, New York
Performer: Cornell University Orchestra, Chorus and Glee Club; conducted by the composer
New York: Associated Music Publishers, 1974
SEE: B25-B26, B65, B72, B104, B131, B162, B181, B192, B195, B210, B226, B252, B295, B297, B308, B311, B315-B316, B329, B338, B472

W65a. *An American Te Deum* (1976) (45 min.)
For baritone solo, mixed chorus and wind ensemble
Text compiled from the writings of Henry David Thoreau, Ole E. Rølvaag, Otokar Brežina, folk, traditional and liturgical sources.
Commissioned by Louie J., Ella, and Joanne Pochobradsky, to commemorate the 125th anniversary of Coe College and the Bicentennial of the United States
Premiere: 5 December, 1976, Cedar Rapids, Iowa
Performer: Allan D. Kellar, baritone, Coe College Wind Ensemble; Coe Concert Chorale, Cedar Rapids Concert Chorale; conducted by the composer
New York: Associated Music Publishers, 1976
SEE: B21, B28, B49, B60, B66, B77, B84, B129, B151, B264, B299-B300,

B362, B421, B432, B488, B514, B525, B554

W65b. *An American Te Deum* [revised version] (1977) (45 min.)
For baritone solo, mixed chorus and orchestra (3-3-3-3; 4-4-3-1; timp; perc; str)
Premiere: 10 May, 1978, Inter-American Festival of Music, Washington, D.C.
Performer: Carl Gerbrandt, baritone; The Festival Orchestra; Peabody Conservatory Chorus; Morgan State University Choir; conducted by the composer
New York: Associated Music Publishers, 1986
SEE: B28, B301, B317, B447

W65c. *There are from time to times mornings* (1976) (6 min.)
For mixed chorus a cappella
Extracted from W65a
Text: Henry David Thoreau
Premiere: See W65a
Performer: See W65a
New York: Associated Music Publishers, 1982
SEE: B514

W65d. *Drum ceremony* (1977) (2 min.)
For 6 percussionists (timpani, tom-toms, woodblocks)
Introductory movement of W65a or W65b
Premiere: See W65a
Performer: See W65a
New York: Associated Music Publishers, 1978/89

W66. *Three Moravian songs* (1981) (10 min.)
For mixed chorus a cappella
Commissioned by the Holland [Michigan] Community Choir
Text from folk texts
Premiere: 14 March, 1981, Holland, Michigan
Performer: The Holland Community Choir (Calvin Langejans, director); conducted by the composer
New York: Associated Music Publishers, 1982
SEE: B514

W67. *Every day* (1981) (7 min.)
For mixed chorus a cappella
Commissioned by the Ithaca College Concert Choir for the Ithaca College Choir Festival
Text: Henry David Thoreau
Premiere: 14 November, 1981, Ithaca, New York
Performer: Ithaca College Concert Choir; conducted by Lawrence Doebler
New York: Associated Music Publishers, 1983
SEE: B514

W68. *Cantata* (1982) (18 min.)
   For male chorus and brass quintet
   Commissioned by the Wabash College Glee Club, Dr. Stanley
      Malinowski, director
   Texts compiled from the writings of E.A. Robinson, Emily Dickinson
      and Walt Whitman
   Premiere: 20 April, 1983, Wabash College Chapel, Crawfordsville,
      Indiana
   Performer: Wabash College Glee Club and student brass quintet;
      conducted by the composer
   New York: Associated Music Publishers, 1982
   SEE: B511

ARRANGEMENTS

WA1. Herschel, William, 1738-1822. *Sinfonia no.XIV in D major.* [arr. 1962]
   For orchestra
   Premiere: 28 August, 1962, Cornell University, Ithaca, New York
   Performer: Rochester Chamber Orchestra; conducted by the composer
   Unpublished

WA2. Lully, Jean-Baptiste, 1632-1687. *Carnaval, a masquerade.* [arr. 1961]
   For orchestra (ca. 18 min.)
   Premiere: 24 November, 1963, Cornell University, Ithaca, New York
   Performer: Cornell Chamber Orchestra; conducted by the composer
   Kassel [W. Germany]: Barenreiter Verlag, 1968
   SEE: B270

WA3. Lully, Jean-Baptiste, 1632-1687. *Le ballet des muses.* [arr. 1961]
   Excerpts, transcribed and arranged for orchestra (ca. 18 min.)
   Premiere: 13 May, 1979, Cornell University, Ithaca, New York
   Performer: Cayuga Chamber Orchestra; conducted the composer
   New York: Associated Music Publishers, 1978
   SEE: B466

WA4. Delalande, Michel, 1739-1812. *Cantemus Domino.* [arr. 1961]
   Motet for soli, chorus and orchestra (ca. 23 min.)
   Premiere: 5 March, 1967, Cornell University, Ithaca, New York
   Performer: John Ferrante, countertenor; John Burns, tenor; Arthur Neal,
      bass; Cornell Chorus and Chamber Chorus; Cornell Chamber
      Orchestra; conducted by the composer
   New York: Lawson-Gould Music Publishers, 1971
   SEE: B82, B494

WA5.   Delalande, Michel, 1739-1812.   *Afferte Domino*.   [arr. 1967]
Motet for soli, chorus and orchestra (ca. 19 min.)
Not performed
Unpublished

Discography

This list includes all commercially produced discs, whether or not currently available. All recordings are 33 1/3 rpm unless otherwise indicated. "SEE" references, e.g. SEE: B546, identify reviews in the "Bibliography" section.

D1. *Al fresco.* (W59)
Golden Crest Records ATH-5066. 1979
James Forger, saxophone; Michigan State University Wind Symphony and Symphony Band; Karel Husa and Stanley E. DeRusha, conductors.
In: *Compositions of Karel Husa.*
Includes his *Concerto,* for saxophone and concert band [W54a], *Concerto,* for percussion and wind ensemble [W60].
SEE: B546

D2. *Al fresco.* (W59)
Mark MC-5405. 1976
Western Illinois University Wind Ensemble; Karel Husa, conductor.
In: *The beaded leaf.*
Includes works by Robert Linn, Warren Benson, and William Hill.

D3. *Apotheosis of this earth.* (W56)
Golden Crest Records CRS 4134. 1974
University of Michigan Symphony Band; Karel Husa, conductor.
Includes his *Music for Prague, 1968* [W55].
SEE: B538

D4. *Concerto,* for alto saxophone and concert band. (W54a)
Golden Crest 4124. 1970
Tim Timmons, saxophone; Ithaca College Concert Band; Edward Gobrecht, conductor.
Includes Ingolf Dahl's *Concerto,* for saxophone and wind ensemble.

SEE: B538

D5.   *Concerto,* for saxophone and concert band. (W54a)
Cornell University Records CUWE-3. [n.d.]
Sigurd Rascher, saxophone; Cornell University Wind Ensemble; Karel Husa, conductor.
Includes his *Music for Prague, 1968* [W55].
SEE: B483, B538

Concerto, for alto saxophone and concert band SEE ALSO D1.

D6.   *Concerto,* for alto saxophone and concert band. (W54b)
Brewster 1203. [1971]
Frederick Hemke, saxophone; Milton Granger, piano.
In: *The American saxophone.*
Includes works by Ingolf Dahl and Warren Benson.

D7.   *Concerto,* for alto saxophone and concert band. (W54b)
Brewster 1216. 1976
Robert Black, saxophone; Patricia Black, piano
In: *Concert repertoire for saxophone.*
Includes works by Henry Cowell and Jacques Ibert.

Concerto, for percussion and wind ensemble (W57) SEE D1.

Czech duets (W3) SEE D10.

D8.   *Divertimento,* for brass quintet. (W13b)
University of Iowa Press. 1976
Iowa Brass Quintet.
In: *Sounding brass.*
Includes works by Eugene Bozza, J.S. Bach, Paul Smoker, Michel Leclerc, Jean Mouret and John Wilbye.

D9.   *Divertimento,* for brass quintet. (W13b)
Golden Crest 4114. [n.d.]
Ithaca Brass Quintet.
Includes works by Verne Reynolds, Mikołaj Zieleński and Andreas Berger.
SEE: B514

D10.   *Eight Czech duets,* for piano, 4-hands. (W3)
Orion 81412. [1981]
Frederic Schoettler and Theresa Dye, pianists.
Recorded in the Carl F.W. Ludwig Recital Hall, Kent State University.
Includes works by Aaron Copland and Robert Starer.

Elegie (W4) SEE D24.

D11.   *Elegie et rondeau,* for saxophone and piano. (W14)
Brewster 1295. [n.d.]

Joseph Wytko, saxophone; Madeline Williamson, piano.
In: *Recital music for saxophone.*
Includes works by Ryo Noda, Tommy Joe Anderson, Leslie Bassett, and
Hermann Reutter.

D12. *Elegie et rondeau,* for saxophone and piano. (W14)
Roncorp EMS-031 [cassette]. 1984
Michael Jacobson, saxophone; Paul Borg, piano.
Includes works by Ingolf Dahl, Warren Benson, and Paul Arma.

D13. *Evocations de Slovaquie.* (W11a)
Grenadilla Records QS1008. 1976
Lawrence Sobol, clarinet; Louise Schulman, viola; Timothy Eddy,
violoncello.
Includes Alan Hovanhess' *Firdausi.*
SEE: B139, B367

D14. *Fantasies,* for orchestra. (W35)
Cornell University Records N80P-5536. [1962]
Orchestre des Solistes de Paris, Karel Husa, conductor.
Includes Robert Palmer's *Memorial music.*
SEE: B118, B538

D15. *Fantasies,* for orchestra. (W35)
Grenadilla GSC 1054 [cassette]. 1984
Orchestres de Solistes de Paris, Karel Husa, conductor.
Includes Sidney Hodkinson's *The edge of the olde one.*

Fantasies SEE ALSO D29.

D16. *Four little pieces,* for chamber orchestra. (W34)
Opus One 51. 1979?
Chamber Orchestra of Albuquerque; David Oberg, conductor.
Includes works by Michael Mauldin and John Robb.

D17. *Landscapes.* (W18)
Composers Recordings CRI SD 192(78). 1978
Western Brass Quintet.
In: *Brass Etcetera.*
Includes Herbert Haufrecht's *Symphony for brass and timpani*

Little pieces (W34) SEE D16

Moravian songs (W62) SEE D31.

D18. *Mosaïques.* (W38)
Composers Recordings CRI USD 221. 1968
Stockholm Radio Symphony Orchestra; Karel Husa, conductor.
Includes works by Alan Hovhaness and Willard Straight.
SEE: B109, B356, B538

D19. *Music for Prague, 1968.* (W55)
Franco Columbo Publications BP 136. 197?
University of Texas Symphonic Band; Karel Husa, conductor.
Includes works by Vaclav Nelhybel and Edward J. Madden.
Educational record reference library series.

D20. *Music for Prague, 1968.* (W55)
Mark Records UMC 2389. 1970
Ohio State University Symphonic Band; Gene Thrailkill, conductor.
Includes works by Vaclav Nelhybel, Alfred H. Bartles and Dmitri
   Shostakovich.
SEE: B91

D21. *Music for Prague, 1968.* (W55)
CBS MK 44916 [compact disc]. 1989.
Eastman Wind Ensemble; Donald Hunsberger, conductor.
Includes works by Ralph Vaughan Williams, Paul Hindemith and Aaron
   Copland.
SEE: B515, B538

Music for Prague, 1968 (W55) SEE ALSO D3.

Music for Prague, 1968 (W55) SEE ALSO D5.

D22. *Music for Prague, 1968.* (W41)
Louisville LS 722. 1972
Louisville Orchestra; Jorge Mester, conductor.
Includes works by Krzysztof Penderecki and Gene Gutché.
SEE: B91, B211

Nocturne (from W35) SEE D29.

Preludes, for flute, clarinet and bassoon (W15) SEE D32.

Serenade, for woodwind quintet, with strings, harp and xylophone (W39) SEE
   D29.

D23. *Sonata a tre,* for violin, clarinet and piano. (W22)
Crystal Records S648. 1986
The Verdehr Trio.
Includes Joseph Haydn's *Three trios,* Hob. IV.
SEE: B107

D24. *Sonata,* no. 1. (W2)
Golden Crest CRS 4175. 1978
Mary Ann Covert, piano.
Includes his *Elegie* [W4], *Sonatina,* op. 1 [W1], and *Sonata,* no. 2 [W5].
SEE: B107

D25. *Sonata*, no. 2. (W5)
Grenadilla Records 1025. 1978
Peter Basquin, piano
Includes works by Ingolf Dahl and Dave Diamond.
SEE: B367

Sonata, for piano, no. 2 SEE ALSO D24.

D26. *Sonata*, for violin and piano. (W17)
Grenadilla Records GS-1032. 1978
Elmar Oliveira, violin; David Oei, piano.
Includes Pamela Layman's *Gravitation*, no. 1.
SEE: B354, B484

Sonatina, for piano (W1) SEE D24.

Sonnets by Michelangelo (W42) SEE D33.

D27. *String quartet*, no. 1. (W10)
Leonarda LPI 117. 1983
The Alard Quartet.
Includes Priaulx Rainier's *Quartet for strings.*

D28. *String quartet*, no. 2. (W12)
Everest SDBR 3200. 1971
Fine Arts Quartet.
Includes his *String quartet*, no. 3 [W16].
SEE: B434, B538

String quartet, no. 3 (W16) SEE D28.

D29. *Symphony*, no. 1. (W32)
Composers Recordings CRI SD 261. 1971
Prague Symphony Orchestra; the Orchestre des Soloistes de Paris; Karel
Husa, conductor.
Includes his *Serenade*, for woodwind quintet, with strings, harp and
xylophone [W39], and, *Nocturne*, from *Fantasies*, for orchestra [W35].
SEE: B368, B538

D30. *The Trojan women.* (W46a)
Louisville Orchestra Records LS 775. 1981
Louisville Orchestra; Akira Endo, conductor.
SEE: B514

D31. *Twelve Moravian songs.* (W62)
Grenadilla GSC 1073 [cassette]. 1988
Barbara Martin, soprano; Elizabeth Rodgers, piano.
Includes works by Walter Piston and Alan Hovhaness.

D32. *Two preludes,* for flute, clarinet and bassoon. (W15)
Vox SVBX 5307. 1977
The Dorian Quintet.
In: *The avant garde woodwind quintet in the U.S.A.*
Includes works by Samuel Barber, Arthur Berger, Elliott Carter, Luciano
Berio, Irving Fine, Lukas Foss, Mario Davidovsky, Jacob Druckman, and
Gunther Schuller.

D33. *Two sonnets from Michelangelo.* (W42)
Louisville Orchestra LS 725. 1972
Louisville Orchestra, Jorge Mester, conductor.
Includes Matthias Bamert's *Septuria lunaris.*

D34. *Variations,* for violin, viola, violoncello and piano.
(W24)
Orion ORS 86498. 1986?
The New England Piano Quartette.
Includes Werner Torkanowsky's *Piano quartet.*

Violin sonata (W17) SEE D26.

Bibliography

WRITINGS BY HUSA

B1. "The acceptance of contemporary music." *Symphony news* 23, no.2 (April, 1972): 8-10.

In this article, Husa reflects on the suspiciousness and caution with which each generation receives the music of its composers, and makes suggestions for the programming of new music. "Today's music cannot but express what happens in the second part of the twentieth century. It will be understood by future generations as such, and valued. There should be no doubt in anyone's mind that this is both a historical fact and a cultural necessity."

B2. "Apotheosis of this earth." *Instrumentalist* 28, no.1 (August, 1973): 35-36.

Husa provides some rehearsal and performance comments for his *Apotheosis of this earth* [W56].

B3. "*Apotheosis of this earth* : some thoughts." *Journal of band research* 9, no.2 (1973): 6-9.

In this article, Husa explains the rationale of his composition *Apotheosis of this earth* [W56] and offers some performance suggestions. "The composer hopes that the destruction of this beautiful earth can be stopped, so that the tragedy of destruction--musically projected here in the second movement--and the desolation of its aftermath (the 'postscript' of the third movement) can exist only as fantasy, never to become reality."

B4.   "Concerto for violoncello and orchestra (1988)." *Program*, University of Southern California Symphony, March 2, 1989.

Notes to accompany the world premiere of Husa's *Concerto*, for violoncello and orchestra [W52]. Husa comments: " . . . a concerto is a work in which the virtuostic (and technical) aspect of the solo part as well as the dialogue between the cellist and the orchestra are of great importance. Also, I hope, it will reflect the enjoyment of music making and listening. . . ."

B5.   "Disturbed music lover vs. contemporary composer." *Instrumentalist* 25 (October 1970): 63-64.

Husa's reply to a letter to the editor from a "disturbed music lover," who says: "To me, Husa's writing and that of his ilk is contrived and studied and not viable." Husa says: "New ideas are not clear immediately because we do not voluntarily accept the unfamiliar, new and unexplored not only in music but in all arts. . . ."

B6.   "Foreword," to *New music notation*, by David Cope, ix-x. Dubuque, IA : Kendall/Hung Publishing Company, 1976.

Husa contributed opening remarks to this text on modern musical notation. " . . . a welcome addition to new music and most important tool to composers, performers, and everyone interested in the performance of contemporary music; and hopefully, it will help to codify the exciting new sounds of today."

B7.   "Music for Prague 1968." *The college and university band*: an anthology of papers from the conferences of the College Band Directors National Association, 1941-1975, compiled by David Whitwell and Acton Ostling, 259-266. Reston, Va. : Music Educators National Conference, 1977.

Karel Husa read this paper at the 16th National Conference of the College Band Directors National Association (Austin, Texas, 1971). It was first published in the proceedings of that conference (pp.180-181), and then later included in the above anthology. In it, he outlines the history of his composition *Music for Prague, 1968* [W55], and provides a detailed analysis of the thematic and motivic material used.

B8.   "Problemy desniho skladatele [Problems of today's composers]." *Perspectivy*, February, 1963.

In this article, Husa addresses many of the problems facing today's composer, including unsympathetic audiences and lack of performance opportunities. "More music is carried on than in previous centuries, but percentwise, fewer contemporary compositions [are played]. In the eighteenth and nineteenth centuries, almost only contemporary music was done. . . . Today we have more concerts, but only some 10 to 15 percent of the works performed are by living composers." [Translated from the Czech.]

B9.   "Some thoughts on percussion." *Woodwind world-Brass and percussion* 14, no.3 (June 1975): 28-29+.

In this article, Husa discusses his technique for percussion composition. "I am not writing for percussion in any special way, but in the same manner I would write for any other group (woodwinds, brass or strings)."

B10. "Thoughts on Czech composers." *Music journal* 30 (July, 1972): 32+.

In this article, Husa provides a brief overview of composing in Czechoslovakia from the middle ages to the present. "For hundreds of years the Czech composers have spread into many parts of the world for religious and political as well as pecuniary and professional reasons. They have not forgotten the country they were born in and they have not forgotten the deep source of Czech music. . . ."

B11. "Three dance sketches." *Percussive notes, research edition* 21, no.3 (March, 1983): 36-46.

An article detailing the history of Husa's composition *Three dance sketches* [W19], with extensive harmonic analysis and a suggested set-up for performance. "I have always been intrigued by the immense possibilities of color, rhythm, melodic expression, as well as technical, virtuosic qualities of the percussive instruments."

WRITINGS ABOUT HUSA

Theses and Dissertations

B12. Casey, Robert L. "Serial composition in works for the wind band." Ed.D. diss., Washington University, 1971.

The purpose of this study is to describe, through detailed analysis, those serial techniques which have been used in selected compositions for the wind band and to compare the procedures found in those works with developments in serial composition in general. This study shows that most of the pieces analyzed employed techniques which were formulated early in the development of the system. An exception to this was Husa's *Music for Prague, 1968* [W55], in which it is shown that serial techniques are employed to control non-pitch parameters.

B13.   Davidson, Richard Carlisle. "Analysis of growth in Karel Husa's *Music for Prague, 1968*." M.M. thesis, North Texas State University, 1976.

In this thesis, the author relates four parameters (thematic development, chord tension, tonality and rhythm) to music growth in Husa's *Music for Prague, 1968* [W55].   Davidson determined that movement in the composition is goal oriented, and each parameter contributes in different ways, one providing contrast, another continuity, and another, variety.

B14.   DeSarno, Ruth Ethel.   "Preparation and performance of *Concerto for percussion and wind ensemble* by Karel Husa." Document accompanying M.A. project, California State University at Long Beach, 1985.

This paper outlines the preparation for a conducting project: a major work for wind ensemble, Husa's *Concerto*, for percussion and wind ensemble [W57].   The piece was rehearsed during the Fall semester (1984) and performed December 9, 1984.   A formal analysis is included, focusing on the formal designs, compositional techniques, and overall stylistic characteristics of the piece.

B15.   Duff, John Andrew.   "Three works of Karel Husa : an analytical study of form, style, and content." Ph.D. diss., Michigan State University, 1982.

A doctoral document, providing biographical information about Karel Husa and examining in detail three of his compositions: *Fantasies*, for orchestra [W35]; *Concerto*, for alto saxophone and concert band [W54a]; and, *Concerto*, for percussion and wind ensemble [W57].   The analyses focused on the formal designs, compositional techniques, and overall stylistic characteristics of the *Fantasies* and the two concertos.

B16.   Fox, Gregory Carl.   "Performance, conducting, and rehearsal problems in five selected contemporary works for wind band." Ed.D. diss., University of Illinois at Urbana-Champaign, 1986.

This study identifies performance, rehearsal and conducting problems in contemporary wind band compositions ranked as exemplary by conductors. Husa's *Al fresco* [W59] was examined, in addition to works by Robert Linn, Warren Bell, Fischer Tull and John Barnes Chance.   Included is a list of 85 exemplary contemporary works for wind band, developed from a 3-phased survey of a panel of 23 expert high school, college and university band conductors.

B17. Hestekin, Kjellrun Kristine. "Structural elements in Karel Husa's *Apotheosis of this earth* (1970)." M.M. thesis, University of Wisconsin/Madison, 1976.

Using examples and illustrations drawn from the band version of *Apotheosis of this earth* [W56], this study shows some of the devices Husa uses to structure each movement within the work. In addition, the means used to construct smaller areas within the context of a movement, as well as formal aspects of the work are considered.

B18. Impola, Crystal. "An analysis of *Concerto for saxophone and concert band* by Karel Husa." M.A. thesis, Eastern Michigan University, 1978.

In an analysis of Husa's *Concerto*, for alto saxophone and concert band [W54a], the author identifies many compositional techniques which reflect the characteristics of Husa's style, including use of the 12-tone row and strong motivic development. In chapters discussing form, linear and vertical organization, texture and timbre, Impola examines the composer's use of both traditional and contemporary methods.

B19. McLaurin, Donald Malcolm. "The life and works of Karel Husa with emphasis on the significance of his contribution to the wind band." Ph.D. diss., Florida State University, 1985.

This dissertation provides information on the life, education and works of Karel Husa with attention focused on his contributions to music in general and to the wind band in particular. The study presents biographical information chronologically and includes information on all of Husa's compositions. Further, McLaurin provides a more detailed discussion of the works for wind band, a listing of works by media, a discography, and a comprehensive bibliography.

B20. Stanley, Bill Thaddeus. "Style elements in selected orchestra works of Karel Husa." M.M. thesis, University of Kentucky, 1975.

This paper studies the stylistic aspects of two early orchestral works of Husa: *Fresque*, for orchestra (W29b) and the *Symphony*, no.1 [W32]. These works were chosen to investigate early style traits, uncluding a study of the orchestration. Elements taken into consideration are melody, meter and rhythm, harmony, texture, form and orchestration.

B21. Tam, Angela Ching-Chi. "Karel Husa : an American Te Deum." D.M.A. thesis, University of Cincinnati, 1986.

An analytical study of Husa's *An American Te Deum* [W65], intended to deepen textual and musical understanding of the work, and as an aid to rehearsal and score preparation. Includes a brief biography and a list of the choral works.

B22. Theurer, Britton E. "Music for trumpet and wind ensemble." D.M. diss., Florida State University, 1988.

This treatise presents structural analyses of the first movements from three twentieth-century trumpet and wind concertos, including Husa's *Concerto*, for trumpet and wind orchestra [W58a].   Includes a bibliography of twentieth-century works for trumpet and wind ensemble.

Books

B23. Boucourechliev, Andre. "Gilbert Gadoffre et la musique à Royaumont." IN: *Vérité poétique et vérité scientifique*, 17-18. Presses Universitaires de France, 1989.

In a chapter discussing Gilbert Gadoffre's contribution to the Royaumont community during 1947-1954, the author notes that Husa was an important figure at this time. "Il n'imaginait pas encore la brillante carrière américaine qu'il devait faire par la suite, mais à Royaumont il fut reçu comme un frère et s'y fit beaucoup d'amis et d'admirateurs." [He didn't yet imagine the brilliant American career he would later have, but at Royaumont, he was treated as a brother, and had many friends and admirers.]

B24. *Conductor's anthology, v.2*: conducting and musicianship, a compendium of articles from *The instrumentalist* from 1946 to 1989 on score study, conducting techniques, rehearsals, and musicianship, 95-101. Northfield, IL: The Instrumentalist Publishing Company, 1989.

Part 1, "Interpretive analyses of band repertoire," includes reprints of articles by Husa [B2] and Byron Adams [B44].

B25. Cope, David H. *New directions in music*, 32-34+. Dubuque, IA: William C. Brown Co., 1976.

Cope mentions Husa's *Apotheosis of this earth* [W56; W64] in several sections of the book discussing modern compositional techniques. Cope concludes: "In *Apotheosis*, one finds the fusion of avant-garde and traditional techniques so complete that neither is visible: a work of unique and personal style."

B26. ----. *New music composition*, 70+. New York: Schirmer Books, 1977.

Cope cites Husa's *Apotheosis of this earth* [W56; W64] as examples for analysis for use of modern compositional techniques.

B27.   Ewen, David. "Karel Husa, 1921-." *Composers since 1900, first supplement*, 153-158. New York: H.W. Wilson, 1981.

A biographical article, including a list of major works and a brief bibliography. "Husa writes functional music and virtuoso music with equal facility and aptitude in styles of 20th century music that meets the demands of the composition."

B28.   Iannaccone, Anthony. "Karel Husa : a composer for his time and beyond." *Cross currents: a yearbook of Central European culture, 1988*, 410-416. Ann Arbor, MI: Dept. of Slavic Languages and Literatures, University of Michigan, 1988. [Michigan Slavic materials ; no.29]

A brief biography of the composer, and criticism of three works: *Concerto, for orchestra* [W49]; *An American Te Deum* [W65 a/b]; *Music for Prague, 1968* [W41]. " . . . they [Husa's works] transcend the ubiquitous labels of conservative and progressive. They are simply the imaginative creations of a major artist who speaks cogently and eloquently to his time and beyond."

B29.   Kendall, Alan. *The tender tyrant: Nadia Boulanger, a life devoted to music*, 66. Wilton, CT: Lyceum Books, 1976.

Husa is listed as a recipient of the Lili Boulanger Memorial Fund's annual award. The fund was organized "to keep alive the memory and music of Lili [Boulanger], and to aid composers of exceptional talent and integrity."

B30.   Kreines, Joseph. *Music for concert band: a selective annotated guide to band literature*, A-11/12. Tampa, FL: Florida Music Service, 1989.

Works by Husa included in the section for advanced bands in this guide are *Apotheosis of this earth* [W56], *Music for Prague, 1968* [W55], and *Al fresco* [W59].

B31.   Manning, Jane. *New vocal repertory: an introduction*, 67-71. London: MacMillan Press, 1986.

An annotated, graded list of 20th-century works in English for solo voice with various accompaniments. Includes an analysis of Husa's *Twelve Moravian songs* [W62]. "To complement the plain melodies the composer has written the most imaginative and varied piano parts which immediately transform the pieces into art songs of a high quality and character; they are satisfying for performers and listeners alike."

B32.   Rosenstiel, Leonie. *Nadia Boulanger: a life in music*, 350. New York; London: W.W. Norton Co., 1982.

Husa is discussed as one of the new generation of composers from eastern Europe who studied with Boulanger.   The author notes Boulanger's admiration for Husa which led to her assistance in helping him obtain a teaching post at Cornell.

B33.   Svejda, Jim. *The record shelf: a guide to the classical repertoire*, 165-66. Rocklin, CA: Prima Publishers, 1988.

The author includes the recording [D3] of Husa's *Apotheosis of this earth* [W56] and *Music for Prague, 1968* [W55] in this guide: "If you've become convinced that Contemporary Music now means either minimalist drivel or incomprehensible noise, you have yet to hear the music of Karel Husa."

B34.   Wolff, Pierre. *La musique contemporaine: l'activité contemporaine*, 312. Paris: Fernand Nathan, 1954.

Under the heading: "Oeuvres et tendances d'aujourd'hui," [Works and trends of today] the author discusses the work of contemporary composers by nationality.   Wolff cites the compositions of Husa in "Les Tchèques," stating "Son ordonnance des douze sons se crée en gammes originales, réalisées par des altérations qui donnent la couleur de ses thèmes, et se conservent dans le développement, dans de souples mutation, vibrantes et souplement sans être rauques." [His twelve-tone sequence is created in original scales, realized by means of alternatives which give the color of its themes and are sustained in the development, in supple mutation, vibrant and yielding, without being harsh.]

Journal and Newspaper Articles

B35.   "76 Bicentennial report (premieres and commissions)." *BMI, the many worlds of music* Spring, 1976: 32-35.

A report of the world premiere of *Monodrama* [W44]. Also mentions some commissions, and the recent premiere of the *Piano sonata no.2* [W5] in Washington, D.C.

B36.   "1980 National Convention, MTNA." *American music teacher* 29, no.3 (1980): 19.

Announcement that Husa would conduct a lecture recital with Mary Ann Covert emphasizing his *Sonatina*, for piano [W1] and *Sonata*, no.2 for piano

[W5].

B37. "1984/85 season premieres". *Symphony magazine* 35, no.5 (1984): 42.

Announcement of the world premiere of Husa's *Concerto*, for orchestra [W49] on April 25, 1985 [premiere was postponed until September 25, 1985].

B38. "1986-87 premieres and season highlights: New York Philharmonic." *Symphony magazine* 37, no.5 (Oct./Nov. 1986): 22.

Announcement of the world premiere of Husa's *Concerto*, for orchestra [W49], commissioned and performed by the New York Philharmonic.

B39. "1987-88 premieres and season highlights: a survey of symphonic celebrations from coast to coast." *Symphony magazine* 28, no.5 (1987): 28.

Announcement of the world premiere of Husa's *Concerto*, for trumpet and orchestra [W51].

B40. "A la B.R.T." *Le Phare du Dimanche*, 14 Feb., 1967.

A review of a concert by the Belgian Radio and Television Orchestra, conducted by Husa and including a performance of his *Symphony*, no.1 [W32]. "On ne peut qu'admirer la maîtrise orchestrale mais il en abuse peut-être ou paraît en abuser faute de la relever par une invention mélodique à laquelle le compositeur paraît, au moins dans cette oeuvre, se refuser." [One cannot help but admire the mastery of the orchestra, but he abuses it, or appears to abuse it, by failing to heighten it by a melodic invention which the composer, at least in this work, seems to refuse.]

B41. Abdul, Raoul. "Cornucopia of rich cultural events." *New York Amsterdam News*, 16 March, 1985, p.23.

A review of the New York premiere of Husa's ballet *The Trojan women* [W46a]. "The score is a major one and deserves a place in the repertory of every major ballet company in the world."

B42. Ackerman, J. Allan. " . . . And many more." *Cornell Daily Sun*, 17 Dec., 1970.

A review of a concert by the Cornell Symphony Orchestra, conducted by Husa and including his *Concerto*, for brass quintet and strings [W40]. "The New England Conservatory Brass Quintet brilliantly matched the high degree of virtuosity demanded of the soloists, and the string ensemble sustained the unbelievable tension evoked with admirable support."

B43.   ----. "Berlioz Requiem outstanding." *Cornell Daily Sun*, 19 April, 1972.

A review of a performance of Berlioz' *Requiem*, by the Cornell Ensemble, conducted by Husa.   "Mr. Husa's flawless reading displayed that consummate skill in marshalling unwieldy forces and penetrating comprehension we have come to expect."

B44.   Adams, Byron. "American composer update." *Pan pipes* 73, no.2 (1980): 32.

A list of Husa premieres and performances for 1980. Includes a list of published scores and recordings. Also notes Husa's service on a National Endowment for the Arts committee and as a judge for the Lili Boulanger prize.

B45.   ----.   "Karel Husa's *Music for Prague, 1968* : an interpretive analysis." *Instrumentalist* 42, no.3 (October 1987): 19-24.

In this article, the author provides an detailed analysis of Husa's *Music for Prague, 1968* [W55] and includes an extensive background of the composition. Adams also notes the major challenges the work presents a conductor. "Every bar . . . is infused with the burning sincerity and compassion of its composer; the interpreter of this masterpiece . . . must come prepared with an equal commitment to the task of bringing the music to life."

B46.   ----.   "The sounds of protest." *Tuning up : a journal for the Philadelphia Orchestra listener* January 1987.

A brief analysis of Husa's *Music for Prague, 1968* [W41]. "Prague becomes a symbol for the sufferings and hopes of the Czech people in Husa's music."

B47.   ----.   "World premiere of a world-class work." *Ithaca Times*, 28 Oct., 1986, p.20.

A review of the world premiere of Husa's *Concerto*, for orchestra [W49]. " . . . The work is a concentrated and impressive artistic statement, containing music of great, at times almost unbearable, intensity of emotion. The performance was a committed, enthusiastic assault upon what is surely one of the most difficult orchestral scores ever written."

B48.   "American music in the University." *Buffalo Philharmonic Orchestra program notes*, May 7, 1966.

Notes accompanying a concert of orchestral music of Elliott Carter, Howard Hanson, Karel Husa (*Mosaïques* [W38]), Leon Kirchner, and Robert Palmer. Includes very brief notes on the works performed.

B49. "'An American Te Deum' -- Coe's anniversary finale." *Coe College Courier* 77, no.1 (January 1977): 2.

An article on the Founders' Day convocation at Coe College which included the world premiere performance of Husa's *An American Te Deum* [W65a]. Also contains an outline of the movements of the work.

B50. " . . . and more music." *Ithaca Journal*, 8 Feb., 1975.

Announcement of a preview concert of Husa's new composition, *Al fresco* [W59], performed by the Ithaca College Concert Band.

B51. Anderson, Jack. "Dance: Louisville Ballet in 'The Trojan women'." *New York Times*, 12 March, 1985, p.C15.

A review of a performance by the Louisville Ballet of *The Trojan women*, with music by Husa [W46a]: "Rumbling and snarling with the drums and trumpets of battle and shivering and sighting with anguish, the music gave the choreography solid support and built to shattering climaxes."

B52. Aponte, Wayne Lionel. "N.Y. Philharmonic presents Professor Husa's concerto." *Cornell Daily Sun*, 18 Sept., 1986, p.3+.

An interview with Husa, prior to the premiere of his *Concerto*, for orchestra [W49]. "To bring out the excellence of each player in the Philharmonic, Husa starts his *Concerto* with the first violinist opening with a solo for several measures. Afterward, the soloist is joined by the leaders of each section. Then, one by one, the players enter until all the strings are involved."

B53. "Apotheosis of this earth." *Program*, The University of Nebraska-Lincoln School of Music, March 5, 1989.

Notes to accompany a performance of Husa's *Apotheosis of this earth* [W56]. Includes a transcription of a taped letter from Husa to the members of the UNL Wind Symphony and a brief biography.

B54. Atta, Barb van. "Husa's music to be featured by Symphony." *Evening Press*

(Binghamton, NY), 27 Feb., 1981.

An announcement of the Binghamton Symphony performance of an all-Czech concert, featuring Husa's *Music for Prague, 1968* [W41], Smetana's *Die Moldau* and Dvorak's *Concerto*, for 'cello and orchestra. An interview with Husa is included: "But sometimes I think 'Why are they only interested in *Music for Prague?*' It is like having six children, but everyone only looks at child number two and says, 'This child is beautiful.'"

B55. ----. "Symphony performance of Husa piece masterful." *Sunday Press* (Binghamton, NY), 1 March, 1981.

A review of the Binghamton Symphony's concert, which included a performance of Husa's *Music for Prague, 1968* [W41]. "Perhaps inspired by Husa's presence in the crowded Forum, every section of the orchestra produced its best and most energetic tones during the Husa piece."

B56. Auer, James. "Concert pays homage to Czech spirit, history." *Milwaukee Journal*, 24 Sept., 1988, p.5A.

A review of a concert by the Milwaukee Symphony Orchestra, including a performance of Husa's *Music for Prague* [W41]. "Husa's curtain raiser, an impassioned, intricately constructed salute to his native city . . . is all conflict and angularity, irony and lamentation."

B57. "Awards and honors and appointments." *BMI, the many worlds of music* 1986, no.1: 58.

Announcment that Husa was awarded an honorary Doctor of Music degree by Ithaca College during its 1986 commencement ceremonies.

B58. Bachmann, Claus-Henning. "Klangsplitter." *Musica* 16, no.1 (1962): 29.

A review of the world premiere of Husa's *Mosaïques* [W38]. "Immerhin zündete sein Stück, eine Uraufführung wie das von Schönbach, auf Anhieb." [His piece is still electrifying, a premiere like that of Schönbach, at the start.]

B59. Bagdon, Robert J. "Parrenin Quartet dynamic." *News American* (Baltimore), 30 Oct., 1969, p.5B.

A review of a concert by the Parrenin Quartet, with Karel Husa as a featured guest. He presented "vocal program notes" concerning his *String quartet, no.2* [W12]. "The Quartet's performances were exciting and dynamic. At times the the sound became a little aggressive, but then so is most of the music of the twentieth century." The concert was the first part of the 20th Anniversary Celebration by the Chamber Music Society of Baltimore.

B60. Baldwin, J. "Drumming around." *Percussive notes* 15, no.3 (1977): 12-13.

A brief note of the premiere of Husa's *An American Te Deum* [W65a], highlighting some important aspects of the work.

B61. Barrett, Marjorie. "Pulitzer Prize offers encouragement to composer." *Rocky Mountain News* (Denver) 4 May, 1977, p.C92.

An interview with Karel Husa, guest artist for the Music Festival at the University of Denver's. He discusses the Pulitzer Prize, his recent commissions and his early musical training. "Any prize gives you a nice feeling. . . . You also develop a feeling that everything you write afterward is immediately being judged and that the judges are twice as hard on you."

B62. Bell, Eleanor. "All Brahms' notes in place." *Cincinnati Post Times and Star*, 27 April, 1968, p.4.

A review of a concert by the Cincinnati Symphony Orchestra, including a performance of Husa's *Symphony*, no.1 [W32]. " . . . one would expect Mr. Husa's musical speech to be French with a Czech accent, or . . . Czech with a French accent. But this . . . has been avoided by Mr. Husa, whose *Symphony* . . . has a very personalized sound that owes nothing . . . to any of the above influences."

B63. Bengel, Tony. "Husa's 2 talents moving, powerful." *Greensboro Record*, 23 July, 1971, p.A9.

A review of a concert by the Eastern Philharmonic Orchestra, conducted by Husa, and including his *Serenade*, for woodwind quintet and orchestra [W39]: "The piece is expertly scored and received a clean, transparent performance", and also his *Symphony*, no.1 [W32]: "Husa's eclectic style molds all its elements into a powerful, personal idiom, at once melodic, dissonant, and strongly rhythmic."

B64. ----. "Karel Husa vitalizes diverse composers." *Greensboro News & Record*, 26 June, 1988, p.C5.

A review of a performance by the Eastern Philharmonic Orchestra, conducted by Husa. "Much of the credit for this sparkling performance goes to Husa. He brought out all of the juicy drama and big crescendos of the Franck, but kept the momentum of the singing line with a disciplined beat that never overindulged in rubato."

B65.   ----. "Philharmonic gives fine performance." *Greensboro News & Record*, 16 July, 1989, p.C6.

A review of a performance by the Eastern Philharmonic Orchestra, featuring a performance of Husa's *Apotheosis of this earth* [W64]: "It is stark and angry, bristling with dense, shrill textures, fierce, thundering outbursts of brass and percussion, atonal and dissonant."

B66.   Benson, Robert E. "Peabody Festival keys off." *News American* (Baltimore), 19 April, 1978, p.5B.

A review of a performance of Husa's *An American Te Deum* [W65a] at the Peabody Conservatory's Festival of American Music and Musicians, conducted by Husa. "Eclectic though it may be, the 'Te Deum' is a work of great theatricality and held the rapt attention of the audience. . . ."

B67.   "Bicentennial report (premieres and commissions)." *BMI, the many worlds of music* Spring 1976: 32-35.

A report of the world premieres of Husa's *Monodrama* [W44] and *Sonata, no.2 for piano* [W5]. The report also notes commissions from the Western Brass Quintet and Coe College.

B68.   Biemiller, Lawrence.   "The compositions of Cornell's Husa: music well-suited for extraordinary times." *Chronicle of higher education*, 9 Sept., 1987, p.B5.

An interview with Husa, who discusses some of his compositions and their inspiration. "If sometime people will say that my music has moved them, . . . and that it's well written, that what's important."

B69.   ----. "A performance in Prague; . . . " *Chronicle of higher education*, 4 April, 1990, p.B7

A report of the Prague premiere of Husa's *Music for Prague, 1968*. A concert was performed by the State Symphony Orchestra on Feb.13, sponsored by the Association of Czechoslovak Composers, and included works by four other composers, which all had a connection to the events in Prague in 1968, but had not been heard in that city.

B70.   Blechner, Mark. "Long Island Chamber Ensemble." *High fidelity/Musical America* 26, No.6 (June 1976): MA25-26.

A review of a concert by the Long Island Chamber Ensemble, including the New York premiere of Husa's *Sonata*, no.2, for piano [W5]. "This sonata, on first hearing, promises to be a substantial addition to the contemporary piano repertoire."

B71. Bletzinger, Andrea. "Pulitzer Prize-winning composer visits campus." *Northwestern weekend* (WI), 24-25 Feb., 1979.

An interview with Husa, conductor for the Lawrence University Symphony Orchestra, Symphonic Band and Concert Choir, including performances of his *Festive ode* [W63], *Music for Prague, 1968* [W41], *Two sonnets from Michelangelo* [W42], and *Apotheosis of this earth* [W56]. "Every child has feelings and sensitivities, but most people don't pursue their natural talent to write poetry, paint or compose music. . . ."

B72. "Bravo for Husa." *Cornell Daily Sun*, 16 April, 1973.

A review of a concert by the Cornell Symphony Orchestra, Glee Club and Chorus and Chorus, featuring Husa's *Apotheosis of this earth* [W64]. "Husa has managed to convey tragedy without indulging in sentimental cliches, has created a vision of doom with artistic integrity instead of a pop harangue."

B73. Bretz, Lynn. "Czech-born composer thrives with music based on experience." *Lawrence Journal-World* (KS), 4 March, 1981, p.8.

Interview with Husa, the featured guest of the 4-day Symposium of Contemporary Music at the University of Kansas. " . . . most of the music I have written myself has come because something has either happened to me in my life or I have seen around me things."

B74. ----. "Evocations of Karel Husa." *Lawrence Journal-World* (KS), 8 March, 1981, p.9B+.

An interview with Husa, who discusses the general public's perception of contemporary music: "People are interested in everything modern, but when it comes to music, . . . their ears are shut, and I don't know why they do it."

B75. Brown, E. (et al.) "Five questions; 35 answers." *Composer* (U.S.) 2, no.4 (1971): 79-88.

An article compiling the answers of seven composers, including Karel Husa, to five questions. Asked if contempory composers write for a small, limited audience, only Husa replied in the affirmative. "New ideas do not attract people fast; they are skeptical; they are not sure what is good in it and frankly, among ourselves (composers), we are not always sure either, but we have to try, we have to go ahead."

B76. Brown, Steven. "Salieri on short end again in competition with Mozart." *Orlando Sentinel*, 2 Feb., 1988.

A review of a concert by the [Orlando] Museum Chamber Orchestra, including a performance of Husa's *Four little pieces* [W34]. "To Karel Husa's *Four little pieces*, with its rich textures and gentle tingles of dissonance, the group brought a dark, full-bodied sound."

B77. "BSU music festival to feature Karel Husa." *Muncie Evening Press*, 1 May, 1979.

Announcement that Husa would be the guest artist for the Ball State University High School Invitational Music Festival. Reports that Husa was scheduled to be the featured speaker at the 24th anual music honors banquet, and would conduct a public concert including his *An American Te Deum* [W65a], *Concerto*, for alto saxophone and concert band [W54a], *Al fresco* [W59], *Divertimento*, for brass and percussion [W13a] and *Serenade* [W39].

B78. Buell, Richard. "Philharmonia: warm, elegant, incisive." *Boston Globe*, 25 Nov., 1974.

A review of a performance by the Boston Philharmonia, conducted by Husa and including his *Portrait*, for string orchestra [W33]. " . . . most of all, Karel Husa's conducting was a realization of one's dreams of how symphonies by Johann Christian Bach and Franz Josef Haydn should go."

B79. Buoy, Jean. "WestConn fest: mostly music." *Danbury News-Times* (CT), 4 March, 1979.

A report of activities at the WestConn Arts Festival which included lectures and workshops by Karel Husa, artist-in-residence at the Western Connecticut State College. Husa also conducted a major performance of his works.

B80. Cariaga, Daniel. "Sidlin conducts in Long Beach." *Los Angeles Times*, 16 Dec., 1980, sect.VI, p.3.

A review of a concert by the Long Beach Symphony, including a performance of Husa's *Music for Prague, 1968* [W41]. "Husa is a composer of strong statement, bold colors and essential songfulness. . . . The . . . work offers little let-up of pressure or heat, and its sharp edges were meant to grate. The full orchestra gave a rousing performance of this striking music."

B81. ----. "USC Symphony introduces Husa concerto at Ambassador." *Los Angeles Times*, 4 March, 1989, sect.V, p.3.

A review of the world premiere of Husa's *Concerto*, for violoncello and orchestra [W52]. "In 23 intense minutes, the concerto progresses from unrestrained hostility to unresolved alienation, brilliantly articulated in orchestral writing of biting neo-expressionism."

B82. Carver, Anthony F. "*Cantemus Domino* / M.R. Delalande, ed. by Karel Husa." *Early music* 5, no.4 (1977): 582.

A review of Husa's edition of Delalande's *Cantemus Domino* [WA4]. "It does not seem to represent the best of Lalande." Carver criticizes Husa's realization of the continuo and ornamentation.

B83. Cauble, Courtenay V. "NHSO soars with superior playing, dynamic unity." *New Haven Register*, 26 Oct., 1989, p.67.

A review of a concert by the New Haven Symphony Orchestra, conducted by Husa and including a performance of his *Trojan women suite* [W46b]. "The piece is effectively atmospheric and evocative, with an impressive orchestration. . . ."

B84. Cera, Stephen. "Peabody Wind Ensemble : Husa's Te Deum." *High fidelity/Musical America* 28, no.8 (August 1978): MA21.

A review of the East Coast premiere of Husa's *An American Te Deum* [W65a]. "The composer's craftsmanship is consistently skillful, but the level of his inspiration varies."

B85. Chapman, Irv. "Husa trumpet concerto opens to rave reviews." *Cornell Chronicle*, 3 March, 1988.

An article noting the successful premiere of Husa's *Concerto*, for trumpet and orchestra [W51], performed by the Chicago Symphony Orchestra, conducted by Sir Georg Solti, with Adolph Herseth, trumpet.

B86. ----. "Husa's concerto has its debut." *Cornell Chronicle*, 2 Oct., 1986.

A review of the world premiere of Husa's *Concerto*, for orchestra [W49]. "Mehta said his colleagues of the orchestra 'have seldom been so taken by the virtuosity of a composition. We experienced the birth of a volcanic isle this evening.'"

B87. ----. "New York Philharmonic to introduce Husa's concerto." *Cornell Chronicle* 18, no.4 (Sept.18, 1986): 1+.

An interview with Husa, prior to the premiere of his *Concerto*, for orchestra [W49]. "Husa said that the concerto . . . contains 'demanding and incredibly challenging passages' which he was moved to write because 'every member of a great orchestra such as the New York Philharmonic is a virtuoso artist.'"

B88. ----. "Organist to perform work commissioned from Husa." *Cornell Chronicle* 19, no.19 (Jan.28, 1988).

A report that Husa would conduct the Festival Chamber Orchestra in a performance of his *Concerto*, for organ and orchestra [W50]. Includes some reviews of the world premiere from Cleveland papers, and announcing some future performances of Husa compositions.

B89. Christie, John. "Texas music educators meet in San Antonio." *Instrumentalist* 39 no.9 (April 1985): 10-12.

A report of the 1985 Texas Music Educators convention, which included a program conducted by Husa. The concert featured his *Smetana fanfare* [W61] and *Concerto*, for wind ensemble [W60]. " . . . the band members responded to Husa enthusiastically, both during the performance and in the ovation."

B90. Church, Francis. "Composer Karel Husa's life of might-have-beens." *Richmond News Leader*, 4 Feb., 1989, p.37.

An interview with Husa, prior to a performance of his *Sonata*, for violin and piano [W17] and *Sonata*, for piano, no.1 [W2]. Husa discusses his life and the forthcoming premiere of his *Concerto*, for violoncello and orchestra [W52]. "The music that has been created in the past 200 years . . . is so solid and well-made, the craft so terrific, that whatever we do today must be judged against these masterpieces. Yet I believe I must put something new and original into what I write. I can't compete with my predecessors."

B91. Close, Roy M. "Husa composition a quality record." *Minneapolis Star*, 3 May, 1973.

A review, as a preview of a Minnesota Orchestra concert featuring Husa's *Music for Prague, 1968* [W41], of the Louisville Orchestra recording of the work [D22]. " . . . the quality of sound on this album is outstanding. 'Music for Prague' is a work that combines many elements, often shoving them together in great dissonant piles of sound, and they come through clearly in this recording."

B92.   ----. "Orchestra reaches peak in 'Music for Prague'." *Minneapolis Star*, 4 May, 1973, p.11B.

A review of a concert by the Minnesota Orchestra, featuring Husa's *Music for Prague, 1968* [W41]. "'Music for Prague' leaves the listener awed by its relentless energy and totally moved by the intensity of patriotic emotion with which it ends."

B93.   Cohen, Paul. "Vintage saxophones revisited: 'classic' band music for the saxophone soloist." *Saxophone journal* March/April, 1989: 8-10.

In this column, the author lists solos for saxophone and band that are proven or well established works in the repertoire. He includes Husa's *Concerto*, for alto saxophone and concert band [W54a] in this list, and concludes: "The impact of the *Concerto* is overwhelming, stunning; cataclysmic. It is a profoundly moving and provacative work that . . . is one of the great 20th century concertos written for any wind instrument."

B94.   "College hosts guest composer." *Ithaca College News*, 9 Sept., 1987, p.2.

An announcement that Joseph Schwantner, first Karel Husa Visiting Professor of Composition at the School of Music would be lecturing at the College. The Professorship was instituted to honor Husa, who retired from the College faculty in 1986.

B95.   Colwill, John. "World's best seemed tired." *Brisbane Courier-Mail*, 21 March, 1988.

A review of a performance by the Chicago Symphony Orchestra on tour in Australia, and including a performance of Husa's *Concerto*, for trumpet and orchestra [W51]. "The slow conclusion that follows a stunningly virtuosic cadenza speaks affirmatively as it radiantly strides forth to meet the end of the 20th century."

B96.   Comerford, Kerry. "Serious composing is alive and well in many places." *Boulder Daily Camera*, 28 March, 1971, p.34.

Article about Husa and a work new to the Boulder Philharmonic repertoire, his *Serenade*, for woodwind quintet, strings, harp and xylophone [W39]. "As a whole, the piece is fresh and unusual and can come under no other heading than that of a new idea."

B97. "Composer honored." *American string teacher* 22, no.2 (1972): 35.

Announcement that two concerts devoted to the music of Husa were presented at Ithaca College. The article notes Husa's recent compositions and appearances as guest conductor of many U.S. and European ensembles.

B98. "Composer Husa conducts his own works for EMF." *Greensboro Daily News,* 22 July, 1971.

Announcement of a concert by the all-professional Eastern Philharmonic Orchestra at the Eastern Music Festival, conducted by Husa, and including performances of his *Symphony,* no.1 [W32] and *Serenade,* for woodwind quintet, strings, harp and xylophone [W39].

B99. "Composers." *Music & artists* 2, no.3 (1969): 42.

Announcement that Husa won the 1969 Pulitzer Prize for his *String quartet,* no.3 [W16], noting the world premiere of the work, and many subsequent performances.

B100. "Composers in focus." *BMI, the many worlds of music* Winter 1976: 23-24.

Biographies of many BMI affiliates whose works were widely performed in the 1974-75 concert season, including Karel Husa. Offers brief information about many of his compositions and awards.

B101. "Composers' panel; Chamber Orchestra." *Ithaca journal,* 18 Nov., 1968.

A review of a concert by the Cornell Chamber Orchestra, part of the Festival of Contemporary Music at Cornell University, including his *Poem,* for viola and chamber orchestra [W36]. "Mr. Husa conducts with impeccable taste, with a lucidity that pulls everything together. He is able to balance any instrumental texture. . . ."

B102. "Concert-goer's news." *Musical events* 24, (August 1969): 27.

Announcement tha Husa won the 1969 Pulitzer Prize for composition, for his *String quartet,* no.3 [W16], noting its future performances in New York and Europe.

B103. "Concert features eminent conductor, soloist." *Singapore American : news of the American community* 23, no.5 (May 1987): 1.

This article provides an introduction to Karel Husa, who was to conduct the Singapore Symphony Orchestra in a performance of his composition *Music for Prague, 1968* [W41]. Quotes *Chicago Tribune* music critic John von Rhein on the work, and lists some of Husa's recent compositions.

B104. "Concert music." *BMI, the many worlds of music* 4 (1973): 37-38.

A report of the premiere of *Apotheosis of this earth* [W64] and the *Concerto, for trumpet and wind orchestra* [W58a]. Also mentions the commission of the *Sonata,* for violin and piano [W17] for the Koussevitsky Foundation.

B105. "Concerto for trumpet and orchestra: Karel Husa." *Chicago Symphony Orchestra program notes,* published for the 1988 Australian tour.

Notes to accompany the Australian premiere of Husa's *Concerto,* for trumpet and orchestra [W51]. Includes a brief biography and some background information on the *Concerto.*

B106. Covell, Roger. "By Georg, it's miraculous." *Sydney Morning Herald,* 19 March, 1988.

A review of a concert by the Chicago Symphony Orhcestra, including the Australian premiere of Husa's *Concerto,* for trumpet and orchestra [W51]. "The composer has complemented the distinctive sound of solo trumpet with sharper-edged orchestral sonorities. Bell-ringing patterns and sounds gave a festive context to a solo line that was more sober than light-hearted. The wooden bubbles of sound produced by a lively xylophone were like an effervescent ingredient in the score."

B107. "Covert plays Husa's piano pieces." *Ithaca College News,* 29 Nov., 1978, p.2.

Announcement of the release of recording of Husa's piano works [D24], performed by Ithaca College faculty member Mary Ann Covert.

B108. Craig, Dale A. "Music: Ithaca College Brass Ensemble." *Ithaca Journal,* 18 Feb., 1960.

A review of the premiere of Husa's *Divertimento,* for brass and percussion [W13a]. "The 'Divertimento' of Karel Husa received a performance worthy of its musical qualities. Of all the works played at the concert, this 'Divertimento' gave the most powerful impression that its unique medium is the brass ensemble."

B109. Croche, Florestan. "New records: three by American composers." *Baltimore Sun*, 2 June, 1968.

A review of a recording [D18], issued by CRI, of works by Alan Hovhaness, Karel Husa and Willard Straight. "Karel Husa's 'Mosaïques' [W38] provide a kaleidoscopic picture of changing sonorities, creative within the individual sections   and in unusual combinations. . . . It is . . . an effective composition, . . . destined to earn a place as one of the important orchestral orchestral works of the Twentieth Century."

B110. Crutchfield, Will. "Concert: The Catskill woodwinds." *New York Times*, 11 June, 1987, p.C15.

A review of a concert by the Catskill Woodwind Quintet, including a performance of Husa's *Recollections* [W23]. " . . . germs of simple intervals and motives, . . . ostinato buildup and sometimes relentless regular rhythms, all lucidly deployed."

B111. ----. "Firkusny plays Dvorak." *New York Times*, 31 Oct., 1988, p.C17.

A review of a performance by the Orchestra of St. Luke's, including the world premiere of Husa's ballet suite from *The Trojan women* [W46b], conducted by Husa.   "The score is full of unusual and well-judged orchestral touches. . . . In general it all sounded like dramatic music composed with a sure hand."

B112. ----. "Verdehr Trio promotes a rare configuration." *New York Times*, 5 March, 1989, sect.1, p.67.

A review of a performance by the Verdehr Trio, including a performance of Husa's *Sonata a tre* [W22]. "The standout was clearly the Husa 'Sonata a Tre,' with its sure sense of climax and dramatic variety in instrumental handling."

B113. Cunningham, Carl. "Veteran performers part of tribute: New York salutes Erich Leinsdorf, Charles Wadsworth." *Houston Post*, 8 May, 1989, p.D-3.

A review of a concert by the New York Philharmonic, including a performance of Husa's *Music for Prague, 1968* [W41]. "The orchestra played the work with a strong sense of commitment, concluding with a deeply moving unison statement of an ancient Hussite hymn to liberty."

B114. Curtright, Bob.   "Karel Husa: stumping for living composers."   *Wichita Eagle-Beacon*, 4 Feb., 1979, p.1C.

An interview with Husa, guest at a concert of the Wichita Symphony, performing his *Fantasies*, for orchestra [W35]. "Husa insists that music of living composers . . . should be a part of every concert--'Even if only for 10 or 15 minutes, so the public will know we exist.'"

B115. "Czech composer Husa to conduct concert." *St. Louis Globe-Dispatch*, 8 March, 1972, p.4N.

Announcement that Husa would lead a series of workshops and conduct 2 special concerts at Washington University, including performances of his *Music for Prague, 1968* [W41] and *Divertimento*, for brass and percussion [W13a].

B116. "Czechoslovakian music to be celebrated at UW." *Wisconsin State Journal*, 19 Oct., 1988, p.2C.

An announcement of the weeklong Festival of Czechoslovakian Music, to take place on the University of Wisconsin-Madison campus, including concerts, recitals, lectures, master classes and open rehearsals. Husa was a scheduled guest of the Festival, to conduct, among other works, performances of his *Music for Prague, 1968* [W41] and *Serenade*, for woodwind quintet with strings, harp and xylophone [W39].

B117. D'Addio, Daniel F. "Karel Husa : *Concerto for trumpet.*" *International Trumpet Guild newsletter* 8, no.3 (1982).

A brief history and analysis of Husa's *Concerto*, for trumpet and wind orchestra [W58a]. "Without question the *Concerto* is destined to become a staple of the solo trumpet repertoire. It is compositionally economical yet quite varied in tonal color and dramatic appeal."

B118. Daniel, Oliver. "Beside Cayuga's waters." *Saturday Review* July 28, 1962: 57.

A review of the Cornell University recording [D14] of Husa's *Fantasies*, for orchestra [W35]. "Husa's three *Fantasies* are imaginative and rewarding. . . . The concluding Nocturne is an exotic and quite delicate impressionistic piece that managed to sound new while avoiding the post-Webernian cliches that have dominated so much contemporary writing. . . ."

B119. Darden, Bob. "Pulitzer composer coming to BU camp." *Waco Tribune-Herald* (TX), 19 June, 1981, p.C1.

Interview with Husa, a guest conductor at the Baylor University Wind Ensemble/Orchestra Camp. In addition to works of other composers, Husa conducted his *Al fresco* [W59] and *Two sonnets from Michelangelo* [W42].

"There is a coterie of artists that did their best work between ages 55 and 75 and I want to be writing then."

B120. Decugis, Claude. "Oeuvres pour saxophone solo." *Magazine de l'Association pour l'Essai du Saxophone* Sept. 1985.

An annotated list of 10 works for solo saxophone and orchestra or band, including Husa's *Concerto*, for saxophone and concert band [W54a]. "Dans un style très personnel, d'une écritue néo-classique, plutôt austère, Karel Husa explore les techniques et les sonorités nouvelles du saxophone, en particulier dans l'aigu, demandant ainsi une haute virtuosité." [In a very personal style, of a rather austere neo-classic idiom, Karel Husa explores the new techiniques and sonorities of the saxophone, particularly in the "aigu", thus calling for a high degree of virtuosity.]

B121. Delacoma, Wynne. "Leinsdorf, CSO masters of contrast." *Chicago Sun-Times*, 12 Dec., 1986.

A review of a concert by the Chicago Symphony orchestra, featuring works by Berlioz, Bartók and Husa's *Music for Prague, 1968* [W41]. "Leinsdorf and the CSO players created a mood of serious intensity from the very first bars. . . . In the final section, . . . the CSO percussion conjured images of erratic gunfire, adding the nervous clamor of bells and drums to the final bars' full orchestral texture."

B122. DeRhen, Andrew. "Chamber music society : Husa premiere." *High fidelity/Musical America* 24, no.7 (July 1974): MA36.

A review of the world premiere of Husa's *Sonata*, for violin and piano [W17]. "The . . . composer . . . seems to have been so preoccupied with writing a rip-roaring, modern-sounding, super-virtuoso showpiece that he neglected to write much music."

B123. ----. "Fine Arts Quartet." *High fidelity/Musical America* 20, (August 1970): 2/14.

A review of a concert by the Fine Arts Quartet, including a performance of Husa's *String Quartet*, no.3 [W16]. "The music is little more than rehashed Bartok with post-Webern cliches."

B124. Dieckmann, Jane. "Handel's Messiah at Bailey Hall." *Grapevine* (Ithaca, NY), 17-23 Dec., 1981, p.26.

A review of a performance of Handel's *Messiah*, by the Cayuga Chamber Orchestra and the Cornell Chorale, conducted by Husa. "The balance between the orchestra and chorus was excellent. . . . Mr. Husa kept the entire ensemble together beautifully and paced the work very well indeed."

B125. ----. "Modern master : the baton of Professor Karel Husa and his compelling music are in demand worldwide." *Cornell Alumni News*, Oct. 1986.

An article about Husa, discussing his life in the United States and his professional connection with Cornell University. " . . . as he explains, the universities and foundations have become the modern patrons for composers. Not only does this patronage offer them a living, but it also keeps them in the musical mainstream."

B126. Diener, Marc. "Disappointing TASHI." *Cornell Daily Sun*, 16 Feb., 1982.

A review of a concert by the contemporary chamber ensemble Tashi, including a performance of Husa's *Evocations de Slovaquie* [W11a]. " . . . brilliantly idiomatic instrumental writing, particularly for clarinet."

B127. Diether, Jack. "Music in the making." *Musical America* 81 (February 1961): 49-50.

A report of the first New York performance of Husa's *Fantasies* [W35] at the second "Music in the making" concert, conducted by Howard Shanet, including works by John Huggler, Daniel Harrison, Eric Stokes and Klaus Egge.

B128. Domeshek, David. "Karel Husa: Composing by Cayuga's waters." *Cornell Countryman* 76, no.1 (October 1978): 16.

An interview with Husa, including some biographical information. Husa discusses composing in an academic environment and his philosophy of composition: "I work more by evolution than by revolution."

B129. Dorsey, John. "Music in praise of America." *Baltimore Sun*, 16 April, 1978, p.D3+.

A review of the east coast premiere of Husa's *An American Te Deum* [W65a] at the Peabody Institute American Music Festival. The composer discusses the work and its inspiration, and his life in Prague under Nazi occupation. " . . . those who go to the performance of 'An American Te Deum,' . . . will hear a work stronger in its affirmation of the continuing promise of America than, perhaps, any native son would be likely to write at this point."

B130. Drake, Elizabeth B. "Berlioz' Requiem, Bailey Hall." *Ithaca Journal*, 17 April, 1972.

A review of a performance by the Cornell Ensemble of Berlioz' *Requiem*, conducted by Husa. "This is certainly the finest performance by . . . these groups, . . . and the total effect was nothing short of thrilling."

B131. ----. "Music by Husa: Ithaca College." *Ithaca Journal*, 11 Dec., 1971.

A review of an all-Husa concert performed by the Ithaca College Orchestra, including his *Four little pieces* [W34], *Music for Prague, 1968* [W41] and *Apotheosis of this earth* [W64]. "The concerts are a tribute to . . . Husa's stature as a composer; they are also a treat to his audience. . . . A clear, powerful performance of a work that becomes more powerful with familiarity."

B132. Duckworth, Manly. "'Music for Prague' played with dedication." *Sentinal Star* (Orlando, FL), 24 Nov., 1977, p.3-B.

A review of a concert by the Florida Symphony Orchestra, at the 6th annual Festival of Contemporary Music at Florida Technological University, featuring a performance of Husa's *Music for Prague, 1968* [W41]. "The music has an uncompromising integrity that gives it an overwhelming impact."

B133. Duerr, Jill. "SSO, Husa Triumph in concert." *Syracuse Post-Standard*, Jan.14, 1978.

A review of a concert by the Syracuse Symphony Orchestra, featuring a performance of Husa's *Music for Prague, 1968* [W41]. " . . . a powerful, emotional, sometimes assaultive piece commemorating a devasting time."

B134. Dwyer, John. "Firkusny, Foss engulfed in warm new spirit." *Buffalo Evening News*, 16 Feb., 1970.

A review of a performance by the Buffalo Philharmonic, including a performance of Husa's *Concerto*, for brass quintet and strings [W40]. "In one way it is in a style and rhetoric no later than . . . Tchaikovsky . . . and with that kind of build-up, though with a sentiment-free discipline and tearless drive. In another way it is quite inventive in its fresh use of known materials and patterns, and if it never signals the presence of an innovator it does suggest the work of a resourceful artistic mind."

B135. ----. "Foss, guest maestros offer gala new-music concert." *Buffalo Evening News*, 9 May, 1966.

A review of a concert by the Buffalo Philharmonic entitled "American music in the University," including a performance of Husa's *Mosaïques* [W38], conducted by the composer. "Not far from tonality, at times, and using some extensions of techniques well worked out earlier in the century, it was a fresh view, nonetheless, of design in motion and color, conveyed with an artistic sense of balance."

B136. Dyer, Richard. "Husa's 'Prague' stirs at BSO." *Boston Globe*, 30 Oct., 1987, p.40.

A review of a performance by the Boston Symphony Orchestra, under the direction of Carl St. Clair of Husa's *Music for Prague, 1968* [W41]. " . . . the piece remains in the repertory because it is powerfully expressive music."

B137. ----. "Karel Husa and the Philharmonia." *Boston Globe*, 23 Nov., 1974, p.30.

A study of Husa as he conducts a rehearsal of the Boston Philharmonia, including brief biographical information.

B138. ----. "Vosgerchian plays Husa--with class." *Boston Globe*, 31 Oct., 1987, p.22.

A review of a performance, by pianist Luise Vosgerchian at Harvard University, of Husa's solo piano music [W1, W2, W4, W5]. Includes a brief discussion of each work. "There were cheers for her . . . and . . . for the beaming composer who had given everyone so much to ponder."

B139. Edwards, Barry. "Husa: Evocations de Slovaquie." *Music magazine* 1, no.3 (May/June, 1978).

A review of a recording [D13] of Husa's *Evocations de Slovaquie*, for clarinet, viola and violoncello [W11a]: "The three movements . . . of this exceptionally fine work are of unalloyed richness of inspiration and contrast."

B140. "Edwin Franko Goldman award." *School musician* 43, no.8-9 (Aug./Sept. 1971): 90.

Announcement that Husa received the Edwin Franko Goldman award, in appreciation for his significant contributions to the literature for concert band.

B141. Elsner, Carmen. "All-star band to be in concert: group to make its debut." *Capital Times* (Madison, WI), 22 Oct., 1989, p.2G.

An announcement that the Wisconsin College All-Star Band, under Husa's direction, would make its debut at the 20th annual State Music Conference.

B142. ----. "Americana enlivens Czech concert." *Wisconsin State Journal*, 17 Nov., 1988, p.8D.

A review of a performance of Husa's *Landscapes* [W18] by the Wisconsin Brass Quintet. "One loved the trombone for its sound effects throughout, the tuba for its fog horn sounds in the second movement and the whole band feeling of all in the final movement."

B143. Emerson, Gordon. "NHSO guest conductor was first a composer." *New Haven Register*, 22 Oct., 1989.

An interview with Husa, guest conductor for a performance of the New Haven Symphony Orchestra. "Composing and conducting do have some common elements, . . . but as a composer you work alone and I like that. . . . And there's the element of discovery (in composing). There's something incredible about finding things that didn't exist until you found them."

B144. "English Brass play Husa in debut." *Ithaca Journal*, 3 April, 1987.

An announcement of the U.S. debut of the English Brass Ensemble, including a performance of Husa's *Landscapes* [W18] and *Divertimento* [W13b].

B145. Ericson, Raymond. "Commissiona steps in to conduct Clevelanders in Husa work." *New York Times*, 19 Feb., 1972, p.21.

A report of a concert in Carnegie Hall by the Cleveland Orchestra, conducted by Sergiu Commissiona, and including the New York premiere of Husa's *Music for Prague, 1968* [W41]. "It is a strong composition, full of ominous contrasts and tension, the drag of slow linear movement, the clash of sustained chords. It is extremely effective on a single hearing. . . ."

B146. ----. "Harris is feted: marks 78th birthday at Long Island Ensemble's revival of 1927 Concerto." *New York Times*, 18 Feb., 1976, p.27.

A review of a concert by the Long Island Chamber Ensemble, including the New York premiere of Husa's *Sonata*, for piano, no.2 [W5]. "On first hearing, it was decidedly effective and stirring."

B147. Everett, Tom, comp. "10 questions: 270 answers." *Composer* 10-11 (1980): 57-103.

The answers to ten questions sent to 27 composers, including Leslie Bassett, Dave Diamond, Lukas Foss, Karel Husa, Vincent Persichetti and others. The composers were asked to cite innovative techniques they use, to comment on the academic situation for composers in America today, to talk about the use of computers in music composition, to discuss the role composer's organizations play in society, and other issues.

B148. Evett, Robert. "Fine Arts Quartet among best." *Star-News* (Washington, D.C.), 6 Sept., 1972.

A review of a concert by the Fine Arts Quartet, including Husa's *String quartet*, no.3 [W16]. "This compelling work is a study in gorgeous quartet textures and commanding thematic material. Some of the music is svelte and elegant, and some of it is brutal. . . . He has created delightful and highly imaginative sonorities to match the drive and intensity of his piece."

B149. ----. "Husa 'Music for Prague' passionate, profound." *Evening Star* (Washington, D.C.), 16 Feb., 1970.

A review of the concert by the U.S. Air Force Band, including works by Kodaly and Karel Husa. "That Husa conducted his own work and nothing else is a pity. . . . His too-few recordings of music by other composers prove that he is one of the few really first-class conductors in the country."

B150. Finn, Robert. "BW's Husa premiere is 'quite an earful'." *Plain Dealer* (Cleveland), 27 Jan., 1973.

A review of a performance by the Baldwin Wallace Conservatory Symphonic Wind Ensemble, featuring Husa's *Apotheosis of this earth* [W56]. "The work made an overwhelmingly powerful impression. . . . The listener is gripped and shaken by this piece."

B151. ----. "Fame doesn't mean fortune, composer tells KSU students." *Plain Dealer* (Cleveland), 24 May, 1978.

A report of a panel discussion with Kent State University faculty members, area music critics and Karel Husa, who rehearsed and conducted a performance of his *An American Te Deum* [W65a] by the KSU Wind Ensemble and University Choruses. " . . . a thoroughly sincere and quite original conception brought off through the professional skill of a gifted composer."

B152. ----. "Quartets by Americans make for expressive main events." *Plain Dealer* (Cleveland), 6 March, 1989.

A review of a performance of Husa's *String quartet*, no.3 [W16] by the Cavani Quartet. "Husa's piece is a work of intense, eerie drama, full of unusual instrumental effects that remind the listener of Bartok and even of George Crumb. . . ."

B153. "First performances." *World of music* 10, no.2 (1968): 74.

A brief notice of the world premiere of Husa's *String quartet*, no.3 [W16].

B154. "First performances." *World of music* 13, no.3 (1971): 84.

A brief notice of the world premiere of Husa's *Apotheosis of this earth* [W56].

B155. "First performances." *World of music* 14, no.4 (1972): 86.

A brief notice of the world premiere of Husa's *Two sonnets by Michelangelo* [W42].

B156. "First performances." *World of music* 14, no.4 (1972): 86.

A brief notice of the world premiere of Husa's *Concerto*, for percussion and wind ensemble [W57].

B157. "First performances." *World of music* 16, no.2 (1974): 79.

A brief notice of the world premiere of Husa's *Concerto*, for trumpet and wind orchestra [W58a].

B158. Fischer, Rebecca. "Concerto for organ and orchestra: Karel Husa (born in 1921)." *Michelson-Morley Centennial Celebration concert (program)*, presented by the Cleveland Institute of Music in conjunction with the Michelson-Morley Centennial Celebration and the Cleveland Museum of Art, Oct.28, 1987.

Notes to accompany the world premiere of Husa's *Concerto*, for organ and orchestra [W50]. Includes brief biographical information, the background of the work and an outline of the composition.

B159. Fleming, S. "Musician of the month : Karel Husa." *High fidelity/Musical America* 19, (August 1969): MA5.

An interview with Husa, who discusses his string quartets [W10, W12, W16] and other compositions. "With No.3 [W16], each player is a virtuoso in himself--I give everyone a chance to hate me!"

B160. Francombe, Leona. "Highlights of the season." *Symphony magazine* 37, no.5 (Oct./Nov. 1986): 19, 22.

An overview of important concerts of the season, including performances of Husa's *Music for Prague, 1968* [W41] by the Chicago Symphony, Philadelphia Orchestra, St. Louis Symphony and Cleveland Orchestra. Also reports the world premiere of Husa's *Concerto*, for orchestra [W49], by the New York Philharmonic.

B161. Frankenstein, Alfred. "Husa: *Fantasies*, for orchestra." *High fidelity/Musical America* 12, no.9 (September 1962).

A review of the Cornell University Records recording [D14] of Husa's *Fantasies* [W35]. "This is one of the most brilliant, exhilarating, expressive and tonic works. . . ."

B162. Freed, Richard. "Cornell University ensembles (Husa)." *High fidelity/Musical America* 23, no.7 (July 1973): MA22.

A review of a Kennedy Center concert by Cornell University Symphony Orchestra, Glee Club and Chorus, including the premiere of the orchestral version of Husa's *Apotheosis of this earth* [W64]. "The music has touches of *2001*, . . . and a few devices already used by Ligeti, Penderecki, Mahler and Holst, but it is thoroughly original in the imaginative use to which these devices are put."

B163. ----. "Husa: Sonata for violin and piano." *Stereo review* 42, no.3 (March, 1979): 92.

A review of a recording [D26] of Husa's *Sonata*, for violin and piano [W17]. "It is an intense and striking work, austere in its language. . . ."

B164. Freeman, Ardith. "Husa premiere 'masterpiece'." *Portland, Maine, Press Herald*, 24 Jan., 1985.

A review of a concert by the New England Piano Quartette, featuring a performance of Husa's *Variations* [W24]. "Separate and together, the instruments . . . build and speak in as many tasteful colors as the instruments can make."

B165. "G. Schirmer/AMP composers in the news." *Schirmer News* 2, no.1 (Winter 1988): 1.

A report of Husa's recent activities, including the world premiere of his *Concerto*, for organ and orchestra [W50] and the forthcoming world premieres of his *Concerto*, for trumpet and orchestra [W51] and *Concerto*, for violoncello and orchestra [W52].

B166. Galkin, Elliott W. "American composers project." *Baltimore Sun*, 24 May, 1968.

A report of the first of 2 concerts in the fourth American Composers Project, by the Baltimore Symphony Orchestra, held at Goucher College, including a performance of Husa's *Poem*, for viola and chamber orchestra [W36]. "Mr. Husa is a musician capable of combining several techniques within a framework which is colorful and passionately insistent, hinting at times at the style of Bartok. He has the gift of elegaic lyricism in the most vital and contemporary of terms."

B167. ----. "Comissiona, DuPre, Husa share satisfying Symphony program." *Baltimore Sun*, 22 Oct., 1970.

A review of a concert by the Baltimore Symphony Orchestra, featuring a performance of Husa's *Music for Prague, 1968* [W41]. "Husa knows how to write idiomatically and elegaically for all instruments and to create a kaleidoscopic pastel of moods and colors. . . . This is virtuoso music, and it received a brilliant performance. . . ."

B168. ----. "A deserving music Pulitzer winner." *Baltimore Sun*, 11 May, 1969.

Announcement of the 1969 Pulitzer Prize award for music, including information about the work [W16] and the composer. "With the award to Husa, . . . recognition has been accorded a musician whose orientation is exquisitely classical and whose language, while original and searching for new means of self expression, can be understood as belonging to the mainstream of compositional practices during the first half of this century." Also includes a brief history of the award, and lists some recipients.

B169. ----. "New, traditional works at Lyric concert." *Baltimore Sun*, 8 Jan., 1974.

A review of a concert of the Baltimore Symphony Orchestra, including the world premiere of Husa's *Serenade*, for woodwind quintet, strings, harp and xylophone [W39]. "This is fresh, dramatic music, in a language hyper-sophisticated, but at the same time natural and spontaneous."

B170. ----. "New York Philharmonic: Husa 'Concerto for orchestra' [premiere]." *Musical America* 107, no.1 (March 1987): 27-28.

A review of the premiere of Husa's *Concerto*, for orchestra [W49], performed by the New York Philharmonic and conducted by Zubin Mehta. " . . . a tour de force, a brilliant fresco of sweeping rhythmic intricacy, meditative lyricism, and constantly changing textures."

B171. ----. "Parennin [sic] Quartet opens Chamber Society series." *Baltimore Sun*, 20 Oct., 1969.

A review of the concert by the Parrenin Quartet, featuring works of Milhaud, Boulez, Lutoslawski, Ravel and Husa. Husa was present at the concert, and discussed his compositional attitudes and convictions.

B172. ----. "Three faces of Romanticism." *Baltimore Sun*, 25 Nov., 1965.

A review of a concert by the Baltimore Symphony Orchestra, including a performance of Husa's *Symphony*, no.1 [W32]. "There is also in this symphony the vocabulary of a composer of today, a musician who has developed his own language and who has the technique to express it with procedures and sounds virtuosic in terms of exploitation of the instruments of the orchestra, both individually and in combination."

B173. ----. "A unique reading." *Baltimore Banner*, 30 April, 1965.

A report on the activities of the Baltimore Symphony Orchestra, in collaboration with invited conductors and soloists at Goucher College, including public readings of works by contemporary North and Latin American composers. "Undoubtedly the most vivid and impressive utterance . . . was that of Karel Husa, . . . who conducted the American premiere of his *Symphony no.1* [W32], a . . . work of monumental proportion and majestic sonority."

B174. Gatz, Carolyn. "Moving 'Trojan women' powerfully evokes war." *Louisville Times*, 30 March, 1981.

A review of the world premiere of Husa's *Trojan women* [W46a]. "Husa's score is a magnificent piece of music, filled with the cacophony and searing pain of war."

B175. Gaul, Jenny. "Wind ensemble presents Husa." *Currents* (University of Rochester) 17, no.15 (April 24, 1989): 9.

An announcement that Husa would conduct the Eastman Wind Ensemble in a concert of his works, including *Apotheosis of this earth* [W56], *Music for Prague, 1968* [W55] and *Smetana fanfare* [W61]. Includes brief background material on the works.

B176. Gee, Harry R. "Music by twentieth century masters, Part 4: Karel Husa and Ned Rorem." *School musician* 57, no.7 (March, 1986): 24.

A review of Husa's *Evocations de Slovaquie* [W11a]. "These characteristic pieces are very alive and intense in expression from the far-reaching elegial contrast of pathless mountains with fantastic vision to the last movement--a wild, frenzied dance and a real tour de force for the clarinetist."

B177. ----. "Une rencontre avec Karel Husa." *Bulletin de l'Association Saxophone Française* 10 (April 1977).

A brief article discussing two of Husa's works for saxophone: *Elegie et rondeau* [W14] and *Concerto,* for saxophone and wind ensemble [W54a]. Gee also mentions Husa's *Two sonnets by Michelangelo* [W42], a work including a substantial saxophone part in the orchestration.

B178. Gelles, G. "Festival: the old and the new." *High fidelity/Musical America* 22, no.12 (December 1972): MA18+.

A review of the Kennedy Center's first music festival, including a performance of Husa's *String quartet,* no. 3 [W16], by the Fine Arts Quartet. "Although it is skillfully crafted and knowing in its effects, it must surely lose interest the second time around."

B179. George, Collins. "Almeida and Quartet show diverse skills." *Detroit Free Press,* 14 April, 1970, p.2-B.

A review of a performance by the Bowling Green State University Quartet at the Detroit Institute of Musical Arts, including Husa's *String quartet,* no.3 [W16]. " . . . if one was appalled at the cacophony at the outset, one was overwhelmed by its force, its vigor and its great sincerity before it ended."

B180. George, Earl. "Easy to understand acclaim of conductor." *Syracuse Herald-Journal,* 14 Jan., 1978, p.8.

A review of a concert by the Syracuse Symphony Orchestra, featuring a performance of Husa's *Music for Prague, 1968* [W41]. "Husa led the orchestra through its multi-colored intricacies in a way that never lost sight of its total effect, which--as usual--was little short of overwhelming."

B181. ----. "Husa thinks big: concert evokes gargantuan sounds." *Syracuse Herald-Journal,* 1 March, 1980, p.12.

A review of a concert by the Syracuse Symphony, conducted by Husa, and featuring his *Monodrama* [W44] and *Apotheosis of this earth* [W64].

" . . . since Husa himself has never been one to stint when it comes to instrumentation in his own music, there were some hair-raising sounds."

B182. Giffin, Glenn. "Husa scores vivid, even monumental." *Denver Post*, 5 May, 1977, p.58.

A review of a concert by the University of Denver Symphony, conducted by Husa and including a performance of his *Two sonnets by Michelangelo* [W42] and *Steadfast tin soldier* [W43]. "The 'Two sonnets' . . . attempts . . . to achieve in sound something of the monumental qualities found in the great works of Michelangelo."

B183. ----. "Symposium in music features composer." *Denver Post*, 17 April, 1982.

An interview with Karel Husa, featured composer of the Celebrity Symposium in Music at the University of Northern Colorado. Husa discussed composing: "It can also be everyday sort of work. Ideas come with construction. There are times when I have to write a commission and when nothing world shaking has happened, nor do I have ideas that I think are incredibly important to say. It is sometimes like playing chess that it is in some way calculated."

B184. Gill, E.J. "Impressive debut for Husa quartet." *Detroit News*, 13 April, 1970, p.3-B.

A review of a performance by the Bowling Green State University Quartet at the Detroit Institute of Musical Arts, which included Husa's *String quartet, no.3* [W16]. "The Husa work, consistently interesting and imaginative, at times stunningly effective, made a strong impression and stimulated the players to their best work of the evening."

B185. ----. "Pulitzer premiere in Detroit." *American musical digest* 1, no.6 (1970): 21.

An excerpt of the above review.

B186. Glickman, Ken. "Composer's career is riding to a crescendo." *Lansing State Journal*, 9 Dec., 1982, 1D+.

An interview with Husa, after the world premiere of his *Concerto*, for wind ensemble [W60] at Michigan State University. The composer discusses his life and the course of his career in composition.

B187. ----. "Husa's new concerto masterful." *Lansing State Journal*, 5 Dec., 1982, p.3B.

A review of the world premiere of Husa's *Concerto,* for wind ensemble
[W60]. " . . . a powerful study of wind instruments--exploring new and
creative ways of blending these sounds together."

B188. Goodman, Peter. "New Husa concerto exciting, substantial." *New York
Newsday,* 27 Sept., 1986, sect.II, p.5.

A review of the world premiere of Husa's *Concerto,* for orchestra [W49].
" . . . the piece is an exciting, substantial work with all the ingredients to
make it a worthwhile addition to the orchestral repertoire."

B189. Granger, Don. "Cellist Harrell proved talented, generous 'Giant.'" *Wichita
Eagle-Beacon,* 5 Feb., 1979, p.10A.

A review of a concert by the Wichita Symphony Orchestra, including
Husa's *Fantasies,* for orchestra [W35]. "The *Fantasies* lie within a narrow
range, dynamically and emotionally."

B190. "Greatest composer?" *Ithaca Journal,* 30 May, 1986.

A brief announcement of a radio program, featuring the music of Karel
Husa.

B191. Green, G. "Current chronicle : Ithaca, New York." *Musical quarterly* 57, no.4
(1971): 660-662.

A report on the third Festival of Contemporary Music at Cornell University,
Nov. 1970, including a lecture by Husa and a performance of his *String
quartet,* no.3 [W16]. "Husa is an experienced orchestral conductor who has
used his ear to amass a storehouse of string resources which really 'sound'."

B192. Greene, Philip. "The Apotheosis: a strong brew." *Ithaca Times,* 5 March,
1980.

A review of a concert by the Syracuse Symphony Orchestra, featuring
Husa's *Apotheosis of this earth* [W64] and *Monodrama* [W44]. "Both *Apotheosis*
and *Monodrama* were effectively played as fierce, tense struggles against
musical forces of destruction. . . ."

B193. ----. "Flying off the Handel." *Ithaca Times,* Dec.6-12, 1979.

A review of a performance of Handel's *Messiah,* performed by the Cayuga
Chamber Orchestra and the Cornell Chorale, conducted by Husa.

"Sometimes conductor Karel Husa simply makes the orchestra dance. . . ."

B194. ----. "Gilels and the CCO: spirits of grandeur." *Ithaca Times*, 18-24 Oct., 1979.

A review of a concert by the Cayuga Chamber Orchestra, featuring soloist Emil Gilels and conducted by Karel Husa. " . . . the special collaboration between Husa and the CCO was at its height."

B195. ----. "Karel Husa stands for freedom." *Ithaca Times*, 21-27 Feb., 1980, sect.2, p.13.

An interview with Karel Husa, who discusses his life and the influences that led him to compose *Apotheosis of this earth* [W56, W64], a work performed by the Syracuse Symphony, under his direction. Asked if he felt the same as when he'd written the work (in 1971), he replied "Yes, . . . even more so today. I somehow feel that the worries . . . I had was not wrong. . . ."

B196. Grey, Gene. "Czech composer's heart in homeland." *Binghampton Press & Sun*, 17 Nov., 1989.

An interview with Husa, recalling the events that influenced his composition *Music for Prague, 1968* [W41, W55]. "You can't make a career out of just a few pieces of music; you must keep writing, probably until you die."

B197. ----. "Musical witness to history." *Binghamton Press & Sun*, 18 Nov., 1989, p.19.

A review of a performance by the Binghamton (NY) Symphony Orchestra, featuring a performance of Husa's *Music for Prague, 1968* [W41]. "That these apocalyptic and historically vital events can be emphasized and commented on with a piece of music is, at once, both remarkable and a testament to an artist's contribution to his own times."

B198. Groark, Steve. "Czech festival concludes on high note." *Wisconsin State Journal*, 21 Nov., 1988.

A review of a concert by the University of Wisconsin (Madison) Symphony in the School of Music "Festival of Czechoslovakian music", including performances of Husa's *Music for Prague, 1968* [W41] and *Serenade*, for strings, harp and xylophone [W39]. "Husa's importance was perhaps nowhere more pronounced than in his effect on the 100 or so students, who got the chance to work with a great visiting conductor and a composer with a lot to say."

B199. ----. "Groups are the same; music isn't." *Wisconsin State Journal*, 9 Dec., 1988.

A review of concerts by the Pro Arte and Fine Arts Quartets, including a performance of Husa's *String quartet*, no.3 [W16] by the Pro Arte.

B200. ----. "Living composers flesh out works." *Wisconsin State Journal*, 16 Nov., 1988.

A review of a concert by the Pro Arte Quartet, including a performance of Husa's *String quartet*, no.3 [W16]. "In this work, Husa has applied a formidable compositional technique to create a work of great tensions and even greater resolutions."

B201. Gross, Daniel. "Pulitzer prize winner Karel Husa still composing after 32 years." *Cornell Daily Sun*, 21 Feb., 1986, p.1+.

An overview of Husa's life and career, highlighting his most famous works--*Music for Prague, 1968* [W41, W55] and *String quartet*, no.3 [W16]. The author writes: "His is the next name on the list of great Czechoslovakian composers: Dvorak, Janacek, Smetana, Martinu . . . Husa."

B202. Guregian, Elaine. "Trumpet concerto receives world premiere." *Instrumentalist* 42, no.9 (April 1988): 38-40.

A report of the world premiere of Husa's *Concerto*, for trumpet and orchestra [W51]. In an interview, Husa discusses the evolution of the work. "Husa says he composed the work with C.S.O. principal trumpet Adolph Herseth in mind, striving to write lines that would show off the player's famous tone, accuracy and unstoppable high range."

B203. Haithcock, M.L. "Karel Husa talks about composing." *Instrumentalist* 36, no.9 (April 1982): 22-25.

An interview with Husa, who discusses various influences on his music, and his studies with Boulanger and Honegger. "What I like in music is the excitement and exaltation of something going on. . . . I am more and more interested in our time. I want to write music of today." The article includes a list of misprints in his *Al fresco* [W59].

B204. Hall, Ellen. "Karel Husa's ballet: a plie for peace." *University of Louisville*

Potential 6, no.24 (March 1981): 12.

An interview with Husa, in which the composer relates some of his ideas behind his ballet *The Trojan women* [W46a]. "I wanted [the audience] to realize that, even though 2,000 years have passed since the fall of Troy, we still have war and killing and no freedom. We think we are so developed because we have invented frozen cakes. But we aren't developed when we kill baby seals and whales for no reason."

B205. Hancock, Elise. "'Composing is not a profession, it's an addiction': the editor eavesdrops at the Peabody Institute, while four master composers attempt to convey their art to the students." *Johns Hopkins Magaine* April 1979: 15-18.

In this article, the author reports on master classes in composition held at the Peabody Institute. Husa, Robert Ward, Hugo Weisgall and Otto Luening listened to student compositions and advised the young composers on various aspects of composition.

B206. Hansen, Donna. "Music Fest: a review." *Northwest Arkansas Times*, 28 July, 1985.

A review of the opening concert of the fourth Music Festival of Arkansas, including a performance of Husa's *Symphony*, no.2 "Reflections [W47]. "*Symphony no.2* is aptly titled 'Reflections', and if the listener considers Husa's background in engineering, painting and music, a great deal about this composition becomes clear."

B207. Harriss, R.P. "A fine concert featuring the strings and woodwinds." *Baltimore News-Post*, 9 Jan., 1964, p.5C.

A review of a concert by the Baltimore Symphony, including the world premiere of Husa's *Serenade*, for woodwind quintet and strings [W39]. "The quintet . . . performed . . . this sprightly and often technically difficult confection very winningly. It is unpretentious but quite attractive. . . ."

B208. Hartley, Mary. "American composer visits Garth Newel rehearsal." *Covington Virginian*, 18 July, 1984.

A report on a rehearsal of Husa's *Variations*, for violin, viola, 'cello and piano [W24], attended by the composer. "A brilliant man who is lavish with his praise, Husa spends his time discussing small points which will enhance the performance."

B209. ----. "Chamber music presented at Garth Newel Sunday." *Covington*

Virginian, 18 July, 1984.

A review of a concert of chamber music at the Garth Newel Music Center, including a performance of Husa's *Variations*, for violin, viola, 'cello and piano [W24]. "In this powerful and moving work, the composer was most articulate in his tonal description of bells . . . of all kinds and sizes. . . . The composer skillfully utilized many of the demanding performance techniques for every instrument. . . ."

B210. Hartzell, L. W. "Karel Husa, the man and the music." *Musical quarterly* 62, no.1 (1976): 87-104.

This article contains a brief overview of Husa's life and a detailed discussion of the development of his compositional processes. Tracing this development from the early works through the composition of *Apotheosis of this earth* [W64], the author emphasizes Husa's attention to pitch detail and tonal balance as characteristic of Husa's musical cohesiveness. Hartzell continues by discussing Husa's exploration of various compositional techniques and concludes with an analysis of the *Apotheosis*. " . . . In *Apotheosis* Husa has brought many of the techniques of his earlier works to their point of culmination. . . . The merits of this composition alone would place Karel Husa among the leading composers of our time."

B211. Harvey, John H. "Minnesota's composition on new recording." *St. Paul Dispatch*, 10 Dec., 1972.

A review of a Louisville Orchestra recording [D22], including Husa's *Music for Prague, 1968* [W41]. ". . . making abundant use of modern techniques, basically represents the continuing current of romanticism. . . . All play a part in evoking the beauties and tragedies of Prague and the enduring spirit of the Czech people."

B212. ----. "'Prague Music' highlight of last concert." *St. Paul Pioneer Press*, 4 May, 1973, p.C43.

A review of a Minnesota Orchestra concert, featuring a performance of Husa's *Music for Prague, 1968* [W41]. " . . . a stunning piece in purely musical terms, but it also is a powerful human expression of nostalgia, anguish and stubbornly held hope."

B213. Haskell, Harry. "Composer's works fuse styles of past, present." *Kansas City Star*, 1 March, 1981, p.1G.

A report of the annual Symposium of Contemporary Music at the University of Kansas, featuring the works of Bartók and Husa. Includes an interview with Husa, a guest of the Symposium. "We cannot throw the past away. . . . As a performer, I like to conduct old music, but also, as a composer, I don't want to forget the past. Practically every composer has roots somewhere. The only one I can think of who really came from nowhere was Charles Ives."

B214. ----. "Husa & Schafer: two composers visit the Midwest; contrasting; each makes its mark." *High fidelity/Musical America* 31, no.8 (August 1981): MA36+

An article on Husa's participation in the Symposium of Contemporary Music at the University of Kansas, including performances of several Husa compositions. "The unifying factor in this diverse body of work is an acute feel for instrumental timbres, balances and formal proportions. It distinguishes Husa as one of our most resourceful and imaginative composers."

B215. ----. "Meeting with a purpose, pleasures of the past: Music Symposium features lesser-known composers." *Kansas City Star*, 15 March, 1981, p.9F.

A report of the Symposium of Contemporary Music at the University of Kansas, featuring the works of Béla Bartók and Karel Husa. "Husa's music is sharp-witted, sophisticated and finely crafted. It is challenging to listen to and perform. By juxtaposing it with music of Bartok and others, the symposium helped place this Pulitzer Prize-winning composer in perspective."

B216. Haskins, John. "Music in Mid-America." *Kansas City Times*, 5 March, 1973.

A report on a 4-day workshop at the University of Missouri at Kansas City Conservatory, conducted by Karel Husa.

B217. Healey, Jon. "He wants his music to move people: Karel Husa to lead NCSA Orchestra." *Winston-Salem Journal*, 5 Dec., 1984, p.13.

An interview with Husa, visiting Winston-Salem to conduct the North Carolina School of the Arts Orchestra in a performance including his *Music for Prague, 1968* [W41]. "To me, personally, music is exciting, music is exhilarating. . . . I want to exhilarate people. When I go to a concert, I like to be swept by something, whatever it is."

B218. Hegvik, A. "Karel Husa talks about his life and work." *Instrumentalist* 29, no.5 (May 1975): 31-37.

Extrapolations from a series of interviews with Husa, in which he discusses his life and the many influences on his compositions. "I heard music in my head, and I thought it was mine. But what I heard was really bits of Beethoven, or Mozart, of whatever else I had been exposed to. If I had been born in China, I would have heard bits and pieces of Chinese music. We take from what surrounds us."

B219. Henahan, Donal. "A Leinsdorf program gives instrumentalists their hour." *New York Times*, 6 May, 1989, sect.I, p.13.

A review of a concert by the New York Philharmonic, including a performance of Husa's *Music for Prague, 1968* [W41]. "The piece, indebted to Shostakovich . . . and others and verging on hollow, extramusical rhetoric music of the time, has nevertheless worn better than most politically inspired works of the 1960's."

B220. ----. "Concert: Premiere of Husa." *New York Times*, 26 Sept., 1986, p.C5.

A review of the world premiere of Husa's *Concerto*, for orchestra [W49]. ". . . a whole genre of such showpieces developed, their primary aim being to show off the orchestra's virtuosity. . . . Mr. Husa's work . . . succeeded in that elementary purpose, but did not go much further, in spite of some fits and starts along its . . . way when the orchestral busywork threatened fleetingly to turn into memorable, meaningful music."

B221. ----. "Woodwinds: Quintet of the Americas." *New York Times*, 27 May, 1980, p.C6.

A review of the New York debut of the Quintet of the Americas, including a performance of Husa's *Serenade*, for woodwind quintet and chamber orchestra [W39]. "The most absorbing performance of the night came in Karel Husa's *Serenade*. . . . This . . . work had little really fresh to say, continually suggesting Bartok and Neo-Classic Stravinsky, but it percolated right along, giving great pleasure with its jaunty rythms and graceful tunes."

B222. Henry, Derrick. "NEC Wind Ensemble creates new believers." *Boston Globe*, 18 Feb., 1984.

A review of a concert by the New England Conservatory Wind Ensemble, featuring a performance of Husa's *Concerto*, for wind ensemble [W60]. "Husa speaks with an arrestingly individual voice, that of a master of sonority and structure, a master . . . with something urgent to express."

B223. "Here and there." *High fidelity/Musical America* 22, no.9 (September 1972): MA29.

A report of the world premiere of Husa's *Concerto*, for percussion and wind ensemble [W57], and, *Two sonnets by Michelangelo* [W42].

B224. "Here and there." *High fidelity/Musical America* 20 (May 1970): 2/8.

A report of the world premiere of Husa's *Concerto*, for brass quintet and strings [W40].

B225. Heuter, Tim, and Chris Martin. "Husa impresses Cap." *Chimes* (Capital University, Columbus, OH) 59, no.23 (April 13, 1984).

A report on Husa's visit to the Capitol University Conservatory of Music.

B226. Higuera, Henry. "Cornell Concert: a new 'Apotheosis'." *Ithaca Journal*, 13 April, 1973, p.6.

A review of a concert of choral music, including Husa's *Apotheosis of this earth* [W64], performed by the Cornell University Symphony Orchestra, Glee Club and Chorus. " . . . although Husa has dared to be grand, written to be powerful, the piece is never manipulative or sentimental."

B227. Holmes, Robert. *"Music for Prague, 1968."* *Detroit Symphony Orchestra program notes*, 2/8-10/73: 4-5.

Program notes to accompany a performance of Husa's *Music for Prague, 1968* [W41]. Includes excerpts from the review of the American premiere and Husa's own official annotation for the work.

B228. Honeycutt, Laura. "Husa writes 'the music of today'." *Lawton Constitution* (OK), 2 March, 1983.

An interview with Husa, guest artist at Cameron University's 20th Century Festival. "I would say my music is the music of today. . . . It is driving, like a motor, and at times, romantic. I think it's dramatic. It's pessimistic at times, but mostly optimist [sic]. It's gentle, it's stormy."

B229. Hoover, Jeffrey. "Composer of note: Karel Husa." *Living music* 6, no.2 (Winter 1988): 2.

A brief biography of Husa, highlighting major events, awards and compositions.

B230. Horsley, Paul. "With Husa, the music stems from the man." *Ithaca Journal*,

8 Feb., 1982.

A review of a performance by the Cayuga Chamber Orchestra, conducted by Husa. "Every phrase that Husa draws from his players seems to be just the way he wants it. . . ."

B231. Hruby, Frank.   "Marilyn Horne heads program which holds a Czech surprise." *Cleveland Press*, 27 Feb., 1971, p.A9.

A review of a concert by the Cleveland Orchestra, including a performance of Husa's *Music for Prague, 1968* [W41]. "What looked on the program like just another new work at first glance came off as a very intense, evocative statement. . . . Its power and relentlessness had a curious, paradoxical air about it--even as the event it lamented had almost three years ago."

B232. Hubbard, George R.   "Helen Starr, Dale Brannon dance leads in Balanchine's 'Serenade'." *Courier-Journal* (Louisville, KY), 15 Feb., 1985, p.C9.

A review of the season opening of the Louisville ballet, including a performance of Husa's *Trojan women* [W46a]. "The Louisville orchestra . . . did well by Husa's complex score."

B233. Humphrey, Mary Lou. "Musician for today." *Stagebill* (Chicago Symphony Orchestra), Winter 1988.

An interview with Husa with biographical information and an overview of his compositional output. "Characteristically, his mature scores are firmly rooted in tradition, yet call upon a wide variety of compositional techniques to achieve the desired sonic effect."

B234. "Husa percussion quartet to be premiered at MENC conference in Miami." *NACWPI Journal* 28, no.2 (1979-80): 33.

Announcement that the work NACWPI commissioned from Husa [W19] would be premiered at the 1980 MENC conference. Includes brief biographical information and mentions some important works and conducting appearances.

B235. "Husa to conduct Bandorama concerto." *Herald Times* (Bloomington, IN), 16 April, 1989.

An announcement that Husa would be the special guest of the Indiana University department of bands at the annual Bandorama concert. Includes a brief biography and partial list of works.

B236. "Husa to receive honorary degree at graduation." *Ithaca College News* 8, no.13 (March 19, 1986): 1.

An announcement that Ithaca College would confer an honorary Doctor of Music degree, on the occasion of Husa's retirement from Ithaca College. The Ithaca College Board of Trustees voted to award the degree, noting "Professor Husa will retire from the faculty at the end of the 1985-86 academic year, ending a teaching career during which this internationally renowned composer and educator touched the lives of many Ithaca students with his creative genius."

B237. "Husa will conduct at music festival." *Cornell Chronicle*, 13 Nov., 1986, p.8.

An announcement of a concert, conducted by and featuring the works of Husa, at the 19th Festival of Contemporary Music at Cornell University. The article also announces future performances of works by Husa by major U.S. orchestras.

B238. "Husa's Concerto for orchestra has initial performance." *School musician* 58, no.3 (November 1986): 21.

A report of the approaching world premiere of Husa's *Concerto*, for orchestra [W49]. Includes brief biographical information and some background for the composition.

B239. "Husa's music to highlight contemporary festival." *Cornell Chronicle*, 22 Oct., 1981, p.2.

A report announcing that two concerts devoted to the music of Husa would highlight the fall segment of the 14th Festival of Contemporary Music at Cornell University.

B240. Huscher, Phillip.   "Concerto for trumpet and orchestra: Karel Husa." *Chicago Symphony Orchestra program notes*, Feb.11-13, 1988.

Notes accompanying a concert by the Chicago Symphony Orchestra, featuring the world premiere of Husa's *Concerto*, for trumpet and orchestra [W51]. Along with a brief biography, extensive analysis of the new work is included. "Significant is both the absence of the lower brass and the presence, in a trumpet concerto, of the two orchestral trumpets as well--and Husa makes magical use of them near the end."

B241. Hushagen, Kaaren.   "Syracuse Symphony Orchestra." *Syracuse guide* 31 (March, 1978).

A review of a concert by the Syracuse Symphony Orchestra, featuring a performance of Husa's *Music for Prague, 1968* [W41]. "A more intense performance of the piece could hardly be possible. Husa demanded in both his writing and his conducting a commitment from the players to equal his own, and the Symphony gave it. . . ."

B242. "In the mood for music." *NewsUpdate* (University of Delaware), 11 April, 1988, p.17.

A brief report on a rehearsal of the University of Delaware Wind Ensemble, conducted by Husa and followed by an informal talk.

B243. "In the news." *BMI, the many worlds of music* November 1967: 15.

Reports Husa's impending visit to Buenes Aires, Argentina to conduct the city's Festival series. Also reports on Husa's future conducting engagements with the French Television Orchestra of Paris and the Brussels Symphony, as well as four concerts by the Buffalo Philharmonic.

B244. "In the repertory: Karel Husa." *MadAminA!* 7, no.1 (Spring 1986): 9.

A report of Husa's activities, including lectures at the Universities of Idaho, Nevada and Western Washington performances of his *Music for Prague, 1968* [W41], and recent commissions.

B245. Ingram, Henry Black. "Music review: Eastern Philharmonic Orchestra." *Greensboro News & Record*, 17 July, 1983, p.B9.

A review of the world premiere of Husa's *Reflections--Symphony no.2* [W47], conducted by Husa. "The piece is characterized by abundant experimentation with textures and unusual sound combinations."

B246. Jacobi, Peter. "Fine work, challenging material at Bandorama." *Herald-Telephone* (Bloomington, IN), 20 April, 1989, p.A8.

A review of the annual departmental concert by the University of Indiana bands, including performances of Husa's *Smetana fanfare* [W61], *Al fresco* [W59] and *Music for Prague, 1968* [W55]. "His music is a long way from Sousa. It's terrific music for band, however, offering ensembles and ensembles within ensembles considerable opportunity to test agility, facility and sonority."

B247. Jacobson, R. "Karel Husa." *BMI, the many worlds of music* January 1970: 14.

An article on Husa's *String quartet,* no.3 [W16], with mention of the orchestral premiere of his *Music for Prague, 1968* [W41] and other future plans. The composer states: "Through many long years I have spent time learning, but for the last five or six I have found something which I believe is myself."

B248. "Janacek Mass has dramatic power in series performance." *Buffalo Evening News,* 8 April, 1968.

A review of a concert by the Buffalo Philharmonic Orchestra, conducted by Husa, and including his *Symphony,* no.1 [W32]. "Without the closest traditional reliance, it is nonetheless so clearly a symphony, and so clear on its own terms of fulfilling form, that it comes as . . . a surprise for a work of 1953."

B249. Johnson, Lawrence B. "Karel Husa speaks out for artist, modern music." *Milwaukee Sentinel,* 21 July, 1971.

Interview with Husa, during his residency at the University of Wisconsin--Milwaukee. Husa discusses his *String quartet,* no.3 [W16] and problems associated with performing "new" music. "We adapt to the new colors and new words of contemporary paintings and novels, but the ear still compares the new with the 150-year-old. . . . that's like comparing the 747 to a horse."

B250. ----. "Prague music played stirringly." *Milwaukee Sentinel,* 28 March, 1977.

A review of a concert by the University of Wisconsin--Milwaukee Symphony Band, including a performance of Husa's *Music for Prague, 1968* [W55] and *Divertimento,* for brass and percussion [W13a]. " . . . the composer kept the music's keen underlying intensity clearly before his young players. Clarity and order indeed characterize Husa's conducting as well as his compellingly original music."

B251. Jones, Abe. "Karel Husa returns to EMF as conductor." *Greensboro News & Record,* 24 June, 1988, p.22.

An interview with Husa, who would be conducting the Eastern Philharmonic in a performance at the Eastern Music Festival.

B252. ----. "Musical presentation has earthly concerns." *Greensboro News & Record,* 14 July, 1989.

An announcement that the Eastern Philharmonic Orchestra would perform Husa's *Apotheosis of this earth* [W64]. Includes brief biographical information and some background of the work.

B253. Jones, Robert T. "Classics at core of Czech concert." *New York Times*, 29 April, 1969, p.40.

A review of a Carnegie Hall concert presented by the Czech Academy of Arts and Sciences in America, including Husa's *Elegie et rondeau*, for saxophone and piano [W14]. "The Elegy is somber and atonal, the Rondo angry and flamboyant, with spectacular tour de force writing for the solo instrument."

B254. Kalmann, Frederick. "Czech music festival to continue this weekend." *Daily Cardinal* (University of Wisconsin, Madison), 18 Nov., 1988, p.4.

A report of the activities at the Czech music festival of the University of Wisconsin School of Music, which included lectures by Husa along with performances of his works. Also, a brief review of a concert by the Pro Arte Quartet, featuring a performance of Husa's *String quartet*, no.3 [W16].

B255. Kapr, Jan. "Nase soudoba hudba v Americe." *Hudebni Rozhledy; casopis Svazu ceskoslovenskych skladetelu* 22, no.10 (1969): 317-318.

Article providing information about various Czech-American composers, including Husa, whose works were performed at a recent music festival in Prague. "Karel Husa . . . is a composer of a rather contemplative type with a sense of noble-minded pathos and solid compositional architecture. However, he also does not lack the capability for dramatic tension, as is testified by both of his compositions which were performed in our festival." [Translated from the Czech.]

B256. "Karel Husa." *BMI, the many worlds of music*   Issue 2, 1974: 26.

A brief background of the Pulitzer Prize winner in music. " . . . he compounds elements of the past and present, using his own distinctly individual recipe."

B257. "Karel Husa." *Composers of the Americas* 18 (1972): 53-60.

An article in English and Spanish on Husa, with brief biographical information, a list of works and a discography.

B258. "Karel Husa." *Le Figaro*, 28 Jan., 1966.

A brief review of a concert by the Orchestre National de   L'O.R.T.F., conducted by Husa, and including the French premiere of his *Serenade*, for woodwind quintet, strings, harp and xylophone [W39]. "L'ouvrage est vivant, varié, subtilement folklorique et non pas descriptif, mais évocateur du pays natal. . . . [The work is lively, varied, subtly folkloric and not descriptive, but rather evocative of his native land]"

B259. "Karel Husa: el arte y la tecnica musical de un gran artista." *Informusica* Fall 1987: 49-50.

Article (in Spanish) containing biographical information and a list of compositions.

B260. "Karel Husa: of proclamations and celebrations." *MadAminA!* 8, no.1 (Spring 1987): 4-6.

A report of the many performances and celebrations connected with Husa's 65th birthday. Special notice is taken of the world premiere of Husa's *Concerto*, for orchestra [W49]. "The sizable Lincoln Center audiences that attended the four performances by the New York Philharmonic showed their strongly enthusiastic reactions by rising at the work's conclusion to cheer Husa, Mehta, and the huge orchestra that had displayed such dazzling virtuosity."

B261. "Karel Husa: *Poem*, for viola and orchestra." *ASUC journal of musical scores* 14: 39-73.

A full score of Husa's 1959 composition *Poem*, for viola and orchestra [W36], with a brief background of the work.

B262. "Karel Husa: the mark of a master." *MadAminA!* 6, no.2 (Fall 1985): 8.

A report of some of Husa's recent activities, including a performance of His *Concerto*, for wind ensemble [W60] at the 1985 MENC All-Northwest Conference in Spokane, and the many performances of his recently premiered composition *Variations*, for piano quartet [W24].

B263. "Karel Husa accepts ITG commission." *International Trumpet Guild newsletter* 34 (February 1979): 103.

Announcement of Husa's acceptance of an ITG commission to compose a work for eight trumpets and optional timpani [W20] for the 1980 ITG conference. Includes brief biographical notes and an abbreviated list of compositions and recordings.

B264. "Karel Husa celebration." *Instrumentalist* 31, no.6 (June 1977): 96.

A report of the world premiere of Husa's *An American Te Deum* [W65a] at Coe College, where Husa reveived an honorary Doctor of Music degree.

B265. "Karel Husa commissioned." *Percussive notes* 22, no.1 (1983): 9.

A report that the University of Georgia commissioned Husa to compose a work for symphony orchestra to be performed during the opening bicentennial convocation in October 1984. Includes a list of recent premieres and commissions, and new releases on record.

B266. "Karel Husa from Orient to Occident." *MadAminA!* 8, no.2 (Fall 1987): 13-14.

A report of Husa's Far Eastern tour in the Spring of 1987 to Japan and Singapore.

B267. "Karel Husa in the news." *G. Schirmer Highlights* May 1986: 1+.

A review of Karel Husa's career, including a brief biographical sketch, and highlighting some important compositions and awards.

B268. "Karel Husa named winner Sudler International Wind Band Composition Competition." *Canadian Bandmasters Association journal* May 1984.

An announcement that Husa's *Concerto*, for wind ensemble [W60] was selected as the winning composition in the first biennial Sudler International Wind Band Composition competition. Includes information about the composition and the sponsor of the competition.

B269. "Karel Husa--Pia Sebastiani." *La derniere heure*, 14 Feb., 1967.

A review of a concert by the Belgian Radio and Television Orchestra, conducted by Husa and including a performance of his *Symphony* no.1 [W32]. " . . . il y a dans sa pensée un caractère tourmente qui nous laisse un peu à distance tout en proclamant cependant une grande égalité d'âme." [There is in its thinking a tormented character which leaves us a bit distanced while nevertheless proclaiming a great uniformity of soul.]

B270. "Karel Husa to conduct on Sunday." *Ithaca Journal*, 20 Nov., 1963.

Announcement of a concert by the Cornell University Chamber Orchestra, conducted by Husa, including works by Lully, A. Scarlatti, Britten, Lesur and Mozart. This performance marked the world premiere of Husa's arrangement of Lully's *Carnaval, a Masquerade* [WA2].

B271. "Karel Husa wins coveted award." *School musician* 55 (February 1984): 8.

A report that Husa was awarded the first Sudler International Wind Band Competition prize for his *Concerto*, for wind ensemble [W60].

B272. "Karel Husa wins Pulitzer Prize." *Instrumentalist* 24 (August 1969): 24.

A report that Husa was awarded the 1969 Pulitzer Prize for music, for his *String quartet*, no.3 [W16]. Includes some background information, and a list of significant compositions.

B273. "Karel Husa y la Chicago Symphony Orchestra." *Informusica* 5 (Otono 1988): 67.

A report [in Spanish] of the world premiere and subsequent Australian premiere on tour of Husa's *Concerto*, for trumpet and orchestra [W51].

B274. "Karel Husa's *Concerto for violoncello and orchestra*." *SCI newsletter* 19, no.3 (June 1989): 8.

Announcement of the world premiere of Husa's *Concerto*, for violoncello and orchestra [W52], that Husa was chosen to receive an award from the American Academy and Institute of Arts and Letters, that CBS would be issuing a recording of Husa's *Music for Prague, 1968* [W55] on compact disc, and that Husa's *Smetana fanfare* [W61] was to be published by AMP.

B275. Katz, Ivan. "Czechs and balances." *New Haven Journal*, Oct.30, 1989.

A review of a concert by the New Haven Symphony Orchestra, including a performance of Husa's *Trojan women suite* [W46b]. " . . . contemporary music at its best, and at its most compelling."

B276. "Kennedy Center Friedham awards." *BMI, the many worlds of music* 1983, no.4: 44.

Announcement that Husa's *Recollections*, for piano and winds [W23] received third place honors in the Kennedy Center Friedham awards.

B277. Kenngott, Louise. "Composer Husa: Pucks to Pulitzer." *Milwaukee Journal*, 27 March, 1977.

An interview with Husa, prior to a performance of his *Music for Prague, 1968* [W55] by the University of Wisconsin at Milwaukee Wind Symphony. Husa discusses the composition and the acceptance problems facing today's composers.

B278. Kerner, Leighton. "Soaring and slouching." *Village Voice*, 11 Nov., 1986, p.80.

A brief review of the world permiere of Husa's *Concerto*, for orchestra [W49]. " . . . it's a big, virtuosic, but middle-weight work. . . ."

B279. Khor, Christine. "A Pulitzer-Prize winner lives in fear of deadlines." *Straits Times* (Singapore), 7 May, 1987.

An interview with Husa, in Singapore to conduct performances of the Singapore Symphony Orchestra.

B280. Kilgori, Donna. "Students, music are his life." *Ann Arbor News*, 27 Jan., 1983, p.D5.

An interview with Husa, in Ann Arbor for the Midwestern Conference on Music, where he conducted the Michigan State University Band in a performance of his *Concerto*, for trumpet and wind ensemble [W58a]. "In hearing a work performed by several eminent musicians, they [the students] gain standards of technical and musical excellence that, in competitive society, sets goals beyond anything dreamed of 40 years ago."

B281. Kimball, George H. "Eastman U.N. concert introduces new music." *Rochester Times-Union*, 23 Oct., 1969.

A review of the Eastman School of Music annual United Nations concert, including a performance of Husa's *Music for Prague, 1968* [W55] by the Eastman Wind Ensemble. " . . . the piece conveys certain unmistakeable moods and feelings. . . ."

B282. ----. "Eastman Winds score." *Rochester Times-Union*, 21 Oct., 1972.

A review of a concert by the Eastman Wind Ensemble, featuring Husa's *Concerto*, for percussion and wind ensemble [W57]. "The three-movement work delivered an impression akin to epic drama . . . with astonishing interplays between kaleidoscopic timbres from the varied battery of percussion and wind resonances."

B283. ----. "Philharmonic's guest scores as composer." *Rochester Times-Union*, 8

April, 1968.

A review of a concert by the Rochester Philharmonic, conducted by Husa and including a performance of his *Fantasies*, for orchestra [W35]. "Husa, as a conductor, is a a musician's musician, efficient and direct, and the orchestra played well for him. . . . As a composer, his *Fantasies* represent him very well indeed. . . . In each, Husa proves a craftsman in building distinctive atmosphere."

B284. ----. "Two musicians to remember." *Rochester Times-Union*, 12 Jan., 1973.

A report on a concert by the Rochester Philharmonic, with Husa conducting Dvorak's *Symphony no.9* and his own *Music for Prague, 1968* [W41]. "Husa has achieved all this . . . with a craftsmanlike skill using an austere harmonic scheme and orchestration that accents sharp, brilliant, intensity-building timbres."

B285. Koch, Kathie. "Composer uses music to glorify the earth." *Student Prinz* (University of Southern Missouri), 22 March, 1979.

A report of a University of Southern Missouri University Forum, in which Husa shared his views on the composition of protest music. "'Composers cannot always write something gently and nice, because we are reflections of the 20th century. . . . At times they must address themselves to the cruelty and ugliness of the society they live in.'"

B286. Koplewitz, L. "From pen to podium with new music (six American composers offer suggestions on what works and why)." *Symphony magazine* 33, no.1 (1982): 9-13+.

An interview with six composers, including Husa, who discuss what they hope for from performers and how to increase performances of contemporary works. Husa comments: "An orchestral composer has the responsibility to know his medium well, to the extent of studying the characteristics of the particular ensemble for which he is writing."

B287. Korpell, Herbert S. "Music review." *Cornell Daily Sun*, 7 May, 1962.

A review of a concert by the Cornell Symphony Orchestra, including Husa's *Elegie et rondeau* [W37]. " . . . an impressive piece due to the sensitive working of tone colors in the first movement and agitation and commotion in the second."

B288. Kraines, Warren. "Burge in Bartok, Cornell Orchestra." *Ithaca Journal*, 4 Dec., 1972.

A review of a concert by the Cornell Symphony Orchestra, conducted by Husa. "He has made Cornell's orchestra not only a learning place for future musicians, but also a music-making body in its own right."

B289. Kramer, Jonathan D. "Karel Husa: Music for Prague, 1968." *Cincinnati Symphony Orchestra program notes*, Oct.23-24, 1987.

Program notes accompanying a performance of Husa's *Music for Prague, 1968* [W41]. Includes background information on Husa and the composition of *Music for Prague, 1968*, and some notes by the composer on the work. The author writes: "What separates this composition from most of the experimental works . . . is that these effects are always employed in the service of emotional expression, never for their own sake or for the sake of novelty alone."

B290. Kriegsman, Alan M. "Fine Arts Quartet: what's new." *Washington Post*, 6 Sept., 1972, p.F9.

A review of a concert by the Fine Arts Quartet, including Husa's *String quartet*, no.3 [W16]. " . . . this music is also cognizant of factors other than architectural elaboration and is a lot more amenable to appreciation."

B291. Kyle, M.M. "AmerAllegro." *Pan Pipes* 61, no.2 (1969): 59.

Notice of the world premieres of Husa's *Concerto*, for saxophone and wind ensemble [W54a], *String quartet*, no.3 [W16], and *Divertimento*, for brass quintet [W13b]. Also notes additional performances of the *Concerto* and the *Divertimento* and many other works.

B292. ----. "AmerAllegro." *Pan Pipes* 62, no.2 (1970): 66-67.

Notice of the world premiere of Husa's *Music for Prague, 1968* [W55], and of the over 100 performances of the work planned for the 1969-70 season. Also notes many performances scheduled for his *String quartet*, no.3 [W16] and that the work won the 1969 pulitzer Prize for music. Includes a list of new publications and recordings and guest appearances with many European orchestras.

B293. ----. "AmerAllegro." *Pan Pipes* 63, no.2 (1971): 63.

Notice of the world premiere of the orchestral version of Husa's *Music for Prague, 1968* [W41]. Also notes many performances of this work as well as his *Concerto*, for saxophone and wind ensemble [W54a]. Includes a list of new publications and recordings, and guest appearances on many campuses.

B294. ----. "AmerAllegro." *Pan Pipes* 64, no.2 (1972): 61.

Notice of the world premiere of Husa's *Apotheosis of this earth* [W56] and the American premiere of the orchestral version of *Music for Prague, 1968* [W41]. Also notes many performances of other works. Includes a list of new commissions, publications and recordings.

B295. ----. "AmerAllegro." *Pan Pipes* 65, no.2 (1973): 57.

Notes the many performances of both versions of Husa's *Music for Prague, 1968* [W41, W55] and *Apotheosis of this earth* [W56, W64]. Includes a list of new publications and recordings, and his appearances as guest lecturer and conductor at many U.S. campuses.

B296. ----. "AmerAllegro." *Pan Pipes* 66, no.2 (1974): 57.

Notice of the many performances of Husa's *String quartet, no.3* [W16] as well as his *String quartets, nos.1-2* [W10 and W12]. Includes a list of new publications and recordings, and notes his appearance as guest lecturer and conductor.

B297. ----. "AmerAllegro." *Pan Pipes* 67, no.2 (1975): 59.

Notice of the world premiere of Husa's *Sonata, for violin and piano* [W17]. Also notes many performances of *Music for Prague, 1968* [W41, W55] and *Apotheosis of this earth* [W56, W64]. Includes a list of new publications and recordings, and notes his appearance at many conferences in the U.S. and Europe.

B298. ----. "AmerAllegro." *Pan Pipes* 68, no.2 (1976): 55-56.

Notice of the world premiere of Husa's *Steadfast tin soldier* [W43]. Also notes many performances of *Music for Prague, 1968* [W41 and W55] and *String quartet, no.3* [W16]. Includes a list of new publications, recordings, and commissions.

B299. ----. "Supplement to *AmerAllegro*." *Pan Pipes* 69, no.3 (1977): 26.

Notice of three bicentennial commissions completed by Husa: *An American Te Deum* [W65a], *Sonata, no.2 for piano* [W5], and *Mondrama* [W44].

B300. ----. "AmerAllegro." *Pan Pipes* 70, no.2 (1978): 46-47.

Notice of the world premiere of Husa's *An American Te Deum* [W65a]. Also notes many performances of other compositions of Husa, including broadcasts over NPR and BBC. Lists new publications and recordings, and notes his appearance at numerous music festivals.

B301. ----."AmerAllegro." *Pan Pipes* 71, no.2 (1979): 35.

Notice of the world premiere of Husa's *Landscapes*, for brass quintet W18], and *An American Te Deum* [W65b]. Also notes many performances of other compositions of Husa, and new publications and recordings.

B302. Lambert, Lane. "Composer of classical music takes the Earth as his guide." *Huntsville Times* (AL), 5 July, 1981, p.E1.

An interview with Husa, guest conductor for the Sewanee (TN) Symphony Orchestra. Husa discusses composition in the twentieth century: "A composer cannot always go down to the audience and say 'Well, how much do you know?' and only write music that they will understand. . . . The public is learning, and the process is perhaps slow, but must exist."

B303. Lanier, S. *"Music for Prague, 1968."* *Kansas City Philharmonic program notes,* 1/22-24/74: 21-22.

Notes to accompany a performance of Husa's *Music for Prague, 1968* [W41]. Includes Husa's own notes for the work.

B304. Lazar, Matthew. "'Carmina Burana' at Cornell." *Ithaca Journal*, 22 March, 1970.

A review of a performance of Carl Orff's *Carmina burana*, by the Cornell Symphony Orchestra, the Cornell University Glee Club and Chorus with assorted guest performers, conducted by Husa. "Almost every aspect of the performance shone, and it is difficult to pick out 'outstanding moments.'"

B305. Ledbetter, Steven. "Music for Prague, 1968." *Boston Symphony Orchestra program notes*, Week 4, 1987: 33-37.

Notes to accompany a concert by the Boston Symphony Orchestra, including a performance of Husa's *Music for Prague, 1968* [W41]. " . . . what comes through any performance of *Music for Prague, 1968* is the power and passion of Husa's rhetoric, which, combined with our knowledge of the events implied by the title, make the score immediate and gripping."

B306. Leonard, Arthur. "Husa in his own works." *Cornell Daily Sun*, 26 April, 1971.

A review of a concert by the Syracuse Chamber Players, conducted by Husa, and including his *Poem*, for viola and chamber orchestra [W36], and *Serenade*, for woodwind quintet and strings [W39]. "The *Poem* . . . is a subdued but powerful work, of the type that requires a note-perfect performance to make its point. It received such a performance last evening. . . . The hero of the evening was Husa . . . and his brilliant conducting."

B307. Levin, Monroe. "Notes on music." *Jewish Exponent*, 27 Feb., 1987, p.94.

A review of a concert by the Philadelphia Orchestra, featuring Husa's *Music for Prague, 1968* [W41]. " . . . a kind of musical Guernica, and the use of the piccolo bird call, ominous percussion and brass chorale had a chilling effect similar to that of Picasso's figures."

B308. Lewis, Diane. "WSU guest composer's works aimed at 20th-century sound." *Wichita Eagle-Beacon*, 7 Feb., 1973, p.2A.

An interview with Husa, guest composer, conductor and lecturer at Wichita State University. Husa speaks of composing for the twentieth century: "We live in an age where everyone wants to make his impression fast . . . like Reader's Digest," and discusses the composition of his *Apotheosis of this earth* [W56, W64]: ". . . the composition has some fantastically loud sounds."

B309. Light, Judith. "Modern music interests Husa." *Cornell Daily Sun*, 11 March, 1959.

An interview with Karel Husa, including brief information about his early life and musical training, with some of his views on modern music in general. "To Husa, modern music is an expression of 20th century life, and it's difficult to say it is either good or bad."

B310. Lindeman, Tim. "Cause for applause at EMF." *Triad Style* (Greensboro, NC), 29 June, 1988, p.21.

A review of a concert by Eastern Philharmonic Orchestra, conducted by Husa. "Husa's somewhat unorthodox and unsmooth manner of conducting obviously made sense to the orchestra."

B311. ----. "EMF's vocal excursion." *Triad Style* (Greensboro, NC), 19 July, 1989.

A review of a performance of Husa's *Apotheosis of this earth* [W64] at the World Peace concert of the Eastern Music Festival. "Husa's piece is practically a compendium of techniques available to a contemporary composer. . . ."

B312. Lo, Vivien. "Karel Husa wins his audience over again." *Hong Kong Standard*, 21 Jan., 1981.

A review of a concert by the Hong Kong Philharmonic, conducted by Husa. "Mr. Husa . . . was again responsible for many of the more wonderful moments of music making."

B313. "London debuts." *London Times*, 3 June, 1972.

A review of the London debut of saxophonist Robert Black, whose program included Husa's *Elegie et rondeau* [W14]. "Full of incident, like this composer's string quartets, these two movements underlined that there were few demands Mr. Black's technique could not meet. . . . Other possibilities do exist for this instrument; and Husa confirms it."

B314. Lowens, Irving. "27th Music Fete presents exquisite string concert." *Washington Evening Star*, 4 May, 1970.

A review of a performance by the Bowling Green String quartet, part of the 27th annual American Music Festival at the National Gallery, which included the Washington premiere of Husa's *String quartet, no.3* [W16]. "It is difficult to resist the temptation to call it a masterpiece; certainly it deserves a longer lifespan than most prize-winning works."

B315. ----. "Husa superb." *Washington Star and News*, 16 April, 1973.

A report on a concert in the Kennedy Center Concert Hall by the Cornell Symphony Orchestra, Glee Club and Chorus, including Husa's *Apotheosis of this earth* [W64]. "Karel Husa is not only one of our most important composers--he is also one of the finest conductors in the business today."

B316. ----. "A taste of Husa." *Washington Star and News*, 15 April, 1973.

A report of a concert to be performed by the Cornell University Symphony Orchestra, Glee Club and Chorus, including Husa's *Apotheosis of this earth* [W64]. Lowens discusses Husa's music and its influences. " . . . the ideal sort of eclectic composer, willing to use anything from our musical heritage, but unwilling to put a work forward as his own unless he has added something of his own individuality to it."

B317. ----. "'Traffic jam' on stage causes change in symphony program." *Washington Star*, 11 May, 1978.

A review of a concert in the Inter-American Festival at the Kennedy Center, including a performance of Husa's *An American Te Deum* [W65b]. "It was easily the most impressive work yet performed in the current Inter-American Festival."

B318. Lynch, Kevin. "Husa music focuses on planet." *Capital Times* (Madison, WI), 23 Oct., 1989, p.31+.

An interview with Husa, conducting the Wisconsin College All-star band in his *Apotheosis of this earth* [W56] and *Smetana fanfare* [W61]. Includes brief biographical information and analysis of *Apotheosis*: " . . . reveals how Husa's perspective pivoted from an excited view of outer space to a humbling new view of our own planet."

B319. Mann, Mary. "When a band plays my heart sings." *Northwest Arkansas Times*, 28 July, 1985, p.B1.

A review of the 1985 Music Festival of Arkansas, which included a performance of Husa's *Symphony no.2* "Reflections" [W47]. "It was different and it was Husa. I figured that actually enjoying two out of the three movements of his piece was about all he could or should expect from anyone."

B320. Maraniss, Wendy. "Piano quartet at Barnes: words do not a recital make." *Ithaca Journal*, 9 May 9, 1985, p.7.

A review of a concert by the New England Piano Quartette, including a performance of Husa's *Variations* [W24]. "Husa's music has in every bar the mark of a master. There is a clarity to his writing even when it is complicated: it is not mere noise, it is interesting noise."

B321. Margrave, Wendell. "Symphony Band fine in exciting concert." *Washington Star*, 20 May, 1972.

A review of a concert by the University of Maryland Symphony Band, featuring Husa's *Concerto*, for saxophone and concert band [W54a] and *Apotheosis of this earth* [W56]. "The score is possibly the most exciting band piece I have heard. . . . The scoring is most imaginative and most effective."

B322. Marra, James. "Karel Husa." *Music Review* 45 no.2 (May 1984): 157-160.

An analysis of Husa's *Sonatina*, for piano (W1), *Sonata*, no.2 for piano (W5), and *Monodrama: portrait of an artist*, ballet for orchestra (W44). "A comparison among these . . . works . . . suggests a trend toward indeterminacy, atonality, an expanding timbral palette. . . ."

B323. ----. "Karel Husa." *Saxophone journal* 13 (September/October 1988): 18-21.

An interview with Husa, who reviews his life and career and discusses some of his works. "'I would say it would be starting with the *Third string quartet* [W16] and the *Saxophone concerto* [W54] and *Music for Prague* [W41], that I have left the past composers for the most part. Yet, one cannot leave them completely, you see.'" A discography of works by Husa is included.

B324. ----. "Karel Husa's *Concerto for saxophone* : an analysis." *Saxophone journal* 9, no.4 (Winter 1985): 12-17.

An article intended to familiarize saxophonists with Husa's *Concerto*, for alto saxophone and concert band [W54a] and Husa's style of composition, particularly in the late 1960's. The author also discusses aspects of performance practices applicable to the *Concerto*. Marra concludes: " . . . Husa's *Concerto* is impressive both in compositional technique and expressive impact. It is a work that the saxophonist will find both technically challenging and musically satisfying!"

B325. Marsh, Robert C. "A genuinely imaginative quality found in Karel Husa's work." *Chicago Sun-Times*, 15 Oct., 1968.

A review of the world premiere of Husa's *String quartet, no.3* [W16]. "Husa's modernism is that growing out of the Schoenberg school. What distinguishes this pose of writing a string quartet from many academic works in that tradition is that its best pages have a genuinely imaginative quality."

B326. ----. "Karel Husa scores hit for solo trumpet concert." *Chicago Sun-Times*, 28 Feb., 1988, Arts & Show sect., p.13.

An interview with Husa, following the successful world premiere of his *Concerto*, for trumpet and orchestra [W51]. Husa talks about the work and its influences, and discusses his rationale for composing.

B327. ----. "Solti and the CSO earn raves on concert tour of Australia." *Chicago Sun-Times*, 20 March, 1988.

A report of the Australian tour of the Chicago Symphony Orchestra, with performances including Husa's *Concerto*, for trumpet and orchestra [W51]. Husa comments: "The acceptance of the three concerts in Perth has been incredible. . . . "

B328. ----. "Trumpet triumph: Herseth and Solti dazzle with CSO." *Chicago Sun-Times*, 12 Feb., 1988.

A review of the world premiere of Husa's *Concerto*, for trumpet and orchestra [W51]. "His concerto is fresh, completely ingenious, and precisely the sort of piece to present Herseth, Solti and the CSO at the top of their form."

B329. Maus, Fred. "A review: Orchestra, Glee Club do fine." *Ithaca Journal*, 7 Feb., 1976.

A review of a concert by the Rochester Philharmonic and Cornell Glee Club and Chorus, including a performance of Husa's *Apotheosis of this earth* [W64]. "The piece is powerful, and compares favorably with such comparable contemporary works as Penderecki's *Auschwitz oratorio*."

B330. ----. "Varied, impressive program at Bailey." *Ithaca Journal*, 28 Feb., 1977.

A review of a concert by the Rochester Philharmonic with the Cornell University Chorus and Glee Club, including a performance of Husa's *Steadfast tin soldier* [W43]. "The orchestra played this brilliant music effectively, and Husa's conducting showed the same dramatic and coloristic flair as the music itself."

B331. McCall, Raymond G. "Contemporary 'King David' gets enthusiastic response." *Daily Record* (Wooster, OH), 5 March, 1960.

A review of a performance of Honegger's *King David*, conducted by Husa. " . . . he revealed some subtle rhythmic effects . . . that are not fully evident in the recording conducted by Honegger himself. For once, the shopworn title of Maestro is well deserved."

B332. McLaurin, Donald Malcolm. "Karel Husa's contribution to the wind band." *CBDNA Journal* 4 (Summer 1987): 24-36.

Brief analyses of the many works by Husa for wind band. Includes a list of all wind band works with the history of each work, a chronological listing of the wind band works, and a discography of the wind music.

B333. McLellan, Joseph. "Columbia Pro Cantare." *Washington Post*, 17 Sept., 1988, p.C11.

A review of a performance by the Columbia Pro Cantare with the Music-Crafters, which included Husa's *Serenade*, for wind quintet, strings, harp and xylophone [W39]. " . . . Karel Husa . . . demonstrated . . . that he is a worthy heir of the great tradition of Smetana, Dvorak and Janacek."

B334. ----. "The New Amsterdam." *Washington Post*, 29 Oct., 1982.

A review of the world premiere of Husa's *Recollections* [W23]. "Husa's work achieved both eloquence and the fascination of intricate structures. . . . "

B335. McMahon, William. "Berlioz Requiem: 'Bouquets.'" *Atlantic City Press*, 27 Feb., 1971.

A review of a performance by the All New Jersey Orchestra, Chorus and Band of Berlioz' *Requiem*, conducted by Husa. "For such a large group combined for the first time in Atlantic City, the young players and singers handled [the music] exceptionally well. Attacks were firm and Conductor Husa had them all under control."

B336. McQuilkin, Terry. "Premiere of Husa's cello concerto tonight." *Los Angeles Times*, 2 March, 1989, sect.VI, p.5.

A report on the approaching premiere of Husa's *Concerto*, for violoncello and orchestra [W52], including some background on the work and and interview with Husa. "Writing with Harrell in mind, he sought, he says, to create 'a virtuosic exploration of the cello, and . . . of the instrument's highest register'."

B337. "Meet the ASTA convention clinicians." *American string teacher* 30, no.1 (Winter 1980): 8-9.

A brief biography of Husa, official guest conductor of the ASTA string orchestra, for the premiere of his *Pastoral*, for string orchestra [W45] and a performance of his *Four little pieces* [W34]. " . . . tasteful and inventive works of mature design. . . . "

B338. "Meet the composer: Karel Husa -- *Apotheosis of this earth*." *Instrumentalist* 28, no.1 (August 1973): 35-36.

Husa discusses his composition *Apotheosis of this earth* [W56, W64], explaining its motivation and including an analysis. "I did not expect when I wrote the work that so many ensembles would be able to perform it so well."

B339. Merkling, Frank. "Arts Festival '79 brings Danbury to the fore." *News-Times* (Danbury, CT), 10 March, 1979, p.9.

A review of an all-Husa concert at Western Connecticut State College, including his *Serenade*, for woodwind quintet and orchestra [W39; arr. for woodwind quintet & piano], the overture to his *Divertimento*, for brass and percussion [W13a], *Elegie et rondeau* [W14], *Landscapes* [W18], and the *Concerto*, for percussion and wind ensemble [W57]. "The chaos was controlled, the effect overwhelming, and those present cheered."

B340. ----. "Husa : composer conducts his own electricity." *News-Times* (Danbury, CT), 12 March, 1979.

Interview with Husa and students at Western Connecticut State College, during Husa's brief residency on the campus. "Playing my music may be hard, but writing it is even harder. I always think the next composition will be easier for me. . . . If I can write 10 or 12 measures a day I consider myself lucky."

B341. Miller, Nancy. "Symphony: Concert is for our times." *Milwaukee Sentinel*, 24 Sept., 1988, sect.1, p.7.

A review of a concert by the Milwaukee Symphony Orchestra, including a performance of *Music for Prague, 1968* [W41]. "Husa's means are largely symbolic. But it is a symbolism of the kind that invites the listener to participate, to contribute his or her own imagery, rather than a musical 'program' that by definition prohibits one's participation."

B342. Mintz, Donald. "On giving new music a chance." *Sunday Star* (Washington, D.C.), 18 June, 1967, p.D1.

A report on the Goucher College/Rockefeller Foundation/Baltimore Symphony Orchestra/American Composers Project. "For at least 2 1/2 hours--and sometimes for 5 hours--each day, the [Baltimore Symphony] orchestra and its various conductors worked their way through a variety of American compositions. . . ." Mintz notes the performance of 30 works in 11 days, including 11 world premieres, with some performances conducted by the composer: " . . . Husa . . . is a professional conductor with an exquisite technique and a considerable European reputation."

B343. Mitchell, Donald. "Some first performances." *Musical times* 95 (April 1954): 202.

A review of the premiere of Husa's *String quartet*, no.2 [W12], including a brief analysis. "The quartet was well written, apart from too much parallel movement between the two violins, and might profitably be heard again."

B344. Mitchell, Kevin M. "It takes more than good ideas for composer." *University News* (University of Missouri at Kansas City), 15 Nov., 1984, p.9.

An interview with Husa, in Kansas City to conduct a master class in composition at the University of Missouri. "What we are writing for is a small audience. We simply accept that we cannot compete with Twisted Sister or . . . the Jacksons. The mass of people will always rather listen to the likes of Johnny Cash than contemporary music. We cannot tell the people how fantastic our music is."

B345. Mobley, Mark. "Pulitzer prize-winning composer active as teacher and conductor." *Virginian-Pilot* (Norfolk, VA), 7 April, 1988, p.B1-2.

A report of a pre-performance telephone interview with Husa, prior to a concert of his works in Norfolk, VA. Husa discusses his life and some works, and the frustration he experienced early in his career in getting works performed.

B346. ----. "Recital of emigre's music full of sparkle." *Virginian Pilot and Ledger-Star* (Norfolk, VA), 10 April, 1988, p.B5.

A review of a recital of works by Husa, including his *Divertimento*, for brass and percussion [W13a], *Two preludes* [W15], for flute, clarinet and bassoon and *Sonata*, for violin and piano [W17]. " . . . even though Czech emigre Karel Husa has been on the Cornell University faculty for almost 35 years, his writing is still passionate and communicative. . . . "

B347. Molineux, A. "The elements of unity and their applications on various levels of the first movement of Karel Husa's *Concerto for wind ensemble*." *Journal of band research* 21, no.1 (1985): 43-49.

An analysis of the first movement of Husa's *Concerto*, for wind ensemble [W60]. "This composition . . . is not only exciting through its orchestration and impeccable attention to detail, but clearly demonstrates Husa's continuing commitment to produce carefully constructed compositions."

B348. Monfried, Walter. "Symphony of talent heard at concert." *Milwaukee Journal*, 10 July, 1971.

A report of a concert performed at the Milwaukee Summer Arts Festival, conducted by Husa and including his *Four little pieces* [W34] and *Serenade*, for woodwind quintet and strings [W39].

B349. Monson, Karen. "Festive reunion for Husa music." *Chicago Daily News*, 18 March, 1976.

A review of an all-Husa concert, including his *Divertimento*, for brass and percussion [W13a], *Elegie et rondeau*, for saxophone and piano [W14], and his three string quartets [W10, W12, W16], performed by the Fine Arts String Quartet. "Husa's language has also assimilated more modern techniques and forms, so that one senses a logical progression from the past to the present, with nary a moment of discomfort or regression."

B350. Mootz, W. "Final program was a triumph for Ballet's resident company." *Courier-Journal* (Louisville), 3 April, 1981.

A review of the season's final performance by the Louisville Ballet, including Husa's *Trojan women* [W46a]. " . . . Karel Husa's fine score set the scene without . . . stagy and unnecessary crutches."

B351. ----. "First Grawemeyer award puts U of L on the map." *Courier-Journal* (Louisville), 17 March, 1985, sect.I, p.1.

Announcement of the award of the first Grawemeyer prize to composer Witold Lutoslawski for his *Symphony*, no.3. Includes comments by Husa, a judge for the contest, on the works and the award: "With this gesture. Mr. Grawemeyer takes his place geside the great benefactors of the past . . . like Count Rasoumovsky, Beethoven's friend and patron."

B352. ----. "'The Trojan women' is triumph for Husa, Jones and U of L." *Courier-Journal* (Louisville), 29 March, 1981.

A review of the world premiere of Husa's ballet *The Trojan women* [W46a]. " . . . Husa has written a lengthy tone poem that throbs with the anguish inherent in Euripides' play."

B353. ----. "University of Louisville : Husa's *The Trojan women* (premiere)." *High fidelity/Musical America* 31, no.8 (August 1981): MA23-24.

An excerpt of the above review.

B354. Morton, Bruce N. "Records." *Virtuoso, and Keyboard classics* 1, no.2 (1980): 42-43.

A review of a recording of Husa's *Sonata*, for violin and piano [W17], performed by Elmar Oliveira and David Oei [D26]. Morton discusses the work: "The . . . sonata is long, brilliant, somewhat diffuse, but with a wealth of dramatic musical ideas." His comments on the performance: "The performance is splendid. The many technical feats . . . are tossed off by the violinist with such apparent ease that they are barely noticed."

B355. Morton, Derek Moore. "Scintillating Solti." *West Australian*, 4 March, 1988.

A review of a concert by the Chicago Symphony Orchestra on tour in Perth, Australia, including a performance of Husa's *Concerto,* for trumpet and orchestra [W51]. " . . . Husa's Concerto for trumpet and orchestra is the product of a lively mind, which integrates the solo part closely into the fabric of the ideas."

B356. "'Mosaïques' is released." *Ithaca Journal,* 15 May, 1968.

Announcement of the release of the CRI recording [D18] of Husa's *Mosaïques* [W38]. Includes brief information about the composition.

B357. Mundell, Helen. "Karel Husa: inspiring innovation." *Saturday Ithaca Journal Magazine,* Jan.20, 1979: 1+.

Interview with Karel Husa, discussing methods and rationale for composing. "We cannot go back; we cannot copy the masters. They wrote so well because they invented something--mixing tradition with something new. We have to take the language of the present--it's the present we are describing in novels, painting and in music. Only those who are reflecting the present will survive."

B358. Murphy, George. "Philharmonic, Husa, Steady as a Rock." *Rochester, NY, Democrat and Chronicle,* 16 Dec., 1962, p.11B.

A review of a concert by the Rochester Philharmonic Orchestra, conducted by Husa, featuring works by Vivaldi, Dvořák, Smetana and Copland. "Husa made no particular fuss over the music, presenting it strongly and straightforwardly. His crisp, vibrant reading came as an interesting and most welcome change. . . . "

B359. "Music festival a wonder." *Tallahassee Democrat,* 14 May, 1981, p.4A.

An editorial, praising the Festival of New Music, held at Florida State University, featuring seven concert programs with eight world premieres. Karel Husa was special guest of the festival, which included a performance of his *Apotheosis of this earth* [W56].

B360. "Music festival concert features Husa's music." *Springdale News* (AR), 23 July, 1985, p.4B.

An announcement that the opening concert of the 1985 Music Festival of Arkansas would feature Husa's *Symphony,* no.2 "Reflections" [W47].

B361. "*Music Journal's* 1972 gallery of living composers." *Music journal* 30,

(Annual 1972): 48.

A brief biography of Husa, including a list of some prizes, commissions and major works.

B362. "Musical performance highlights anniversary." *New Cosmos* (Coe College, Cedar Rapids, IA) 86, no.12 (Dec.10, 1976): 1.

A report of the world premiere of Husa's *An American Te Deum* [W65a]. "The . . . performance by the Coe Concert Band, Concert Choir and Cedar Rapids Concert Chorale, was a demonstration of the diversity of the talents of the performers, as well as their abilities to concentrate and relate to the complex and unusual requirements of the piece."

B363. Nelson, Boris. "Feelings expressed musically." *Toldeo Blade*, 13 May, 1979, sect.G, p.1.

An interview with Husa, including brief biographical information and a discussion of his musical style. "Call him a 'Gebrauchmusiker' (practical musician) if you will, but he believes that music should be accessible to all sorts of musicians and audiences without always having to tax and intrigue the select few only."

B364. ----. "Husa conducts BGSU Band in own 'Apotheosis of Earth' : Pulitzer Prize-winning composer focus of evening of contemporary work." *Toledo Blade*, 10 May, 1973, p.30.

Description of a concert of contemporary music by the Bowling Green State University Symphonic Band, including Husa's *Apotheosis of this earth* [W56]. "It is a complicated score, technically masterful and immediately accessible."

B365. Nelson, Judy Ruppel. "Music education in retrospect: an interview with John Paynter." *Instrumentalist* 40, no.1 (August 1985): 12-18.

In an interview with John Paynter, director of bands at Northwestern University, Paynter comments that relationship between prominent American composers, such as Karel Husa, and students of all ages represents a remarkable development in music education that was not possible earlier in this century.

B366. ----. "Karel Husa -- echoing mankind through music." *Instrumentalist* 42, no.3 (October 1987): 12-18.

In this interview, Husa discusses his life, the influences on his compositions and teaching music. "When I was a student at the Prague Conservatory for five years, only two pieces of mine were performed. Here, every term, young composers write music and it is performed. Students can hear what they have written; and that is very important."

B367. Newall, Robert H. "Classical lines." *Bangor Daily News*, 17 May, 1980.

A review of two recordings featuring works of Husa: his *Sonata*, no.2 for piano [W5, D25], and, *Evocations de Slovaquie* [W11a, D13]. "The [*Sonata*], making use of the full resources of the piano, is all music. . . . Peter Basquin, commanding a full tone, makes the most of its massive climaxes and its shimmering pianissimi." Of *Evocations de Slovaquie*, the reviewer comments: " . . . this cunningly devised composition summoning up the composer's recollections of his native land at a particularly acrid moment--a moment . . . when he decided against returning to his country."

B368. ----. "Husa music rated 'brilliant'." *Bangor Daily News*, 23 April, 1977, p.13.

A review of a recording [D29] of Husa's *Symphony*, no.1 [W32], *Serenade*, for woodwind quintet with strings, harp and xylophone [W39] and "Nocturne," from *Fantasies*, for orchestra [W35]. "The music is powerful, original and elegantly orchestrated."

B369. "News nuggets." *International musician* 68, no.4 (October 1969): 11.

Announcement of Husa's 1969 Pulitzer Prize award for music. Includes a list of his other awards and conducting appearances.

B370. "News nuggets." *International musician* 69, no.1 (January 1971): 12.

Announcement that Husa's *String quartet*, no.3 [W16] was staged as a ballet by Denis Nahat with the Swedish Royal Ballet in Stockholm, and notes a future performance by the American Ballet Company.

B371. "News nuggets." *International musician* 72, no.10 (April 1974): 17.

Announcement of the world premiere of Husa's *Sonata*, for violin and piano [W17].

B372. "News nuggets." *International musician* 72, no.12 (June 1974): 13.

Announcement that Ani Kavafian substituted for Jaime Laredo in the world premiere of Husa's *Sonata*, for violin and piano [W17].

B373. Nordheimer, Patricia. "Cornell's Karel Husa wins Pulitzer for music." *Ithaca Journal*, 6 May, 1969.

Report of announcement that Husa had won the 1969 Pulitzer Prize for music for his *String quartet*, no.3 [W16]. Includes biographical information about Husa, with some thoughts on the work and its premiere by the Fine Arts Quartet. "It is a difficult work, and their performance of it is just perfect. . . . The music does not leave behind all the old heritage and tradition of composition, but likewise does not ignore contemporary technique. . . . It is a continuation, a combination, some new, some traditional."

B374. "Notables". *Cornell Chronicle*, 8 June, 1989, p.2.

An announcement that the American Academy and Institute of Arts and Letters presented a $5,000 cash award to Husa, "to honor and encourage composers in their creative work." In addition, Husa received a citation stating that he "is a composer of dramatic utterances, thoroughly of his time, his music breathes and seethes with emotional eloquence. But he goes beyond this and becomes a musical poet of imagination and power."

B375. "Notizen : Uraufführungen." *Das Orchester* 9 (1986): 982.

A notice [in German] of the world premiere of Husa's *Concerto*, for orchestra [W49].

B376. O'Connor, Don. "Husa's energetic score, conducting liven evening." *Syracuse Post-Standard*, 24 April, 1971, p.5.

A review of a performance by the Syracuse Symphony Chamber Players, conducted by Karel Husa, and including performances of his *Poem*, for viola and chamber orchestra [W36] and *Serenade*, for woodwind quintet and string orchestra [W39]. " . . . his craftsmanship is sure and the fragments soon coalesce into recognizable shape. . . . Husa calculates his scoring to the last sixteenth note and it carries well."

B377. O'Leary, Sal. "Very good Wolfgang!" *Cornell Daily Sun*, 17 Sept., 1981, p.11.

A review of a concert in the Cayuga Chamber Orchestra's Mozart Festival, conducted by Husa, featuring Mozart's *Symphony*, no.29 and *Coronation Mass*. "Good taste, confidence, and the respect of one master for another sufficed to sweep the 18th Century masterworks into elevated, penetrating life."

B378. O'Reilly, F. Warren. "The few, the proud, the premiere." *Washington Times*,

19 April, 1982.

A review of a concert by the United States Marine Band, including a performance of Husa's *Concerto,* for wind ensemble [W60]. " . . . a major contribution to the wind ensemble literature. . . . The exciting rhythmic drive makes this music seem faster than it is. Few composers ever enjoy such a polished first performance as . . . was given by the Marine Band."

B379. ----. "Friendship honored by four works." *Washington Times,* 1 Nov., 1982.

A review of the world premiere of Husa's *Recollections* [W23]. "It is a kaleidoscopic melange of melodic ideas treated serially, with controlled aleatorism and occasional instances of conventional harmony."

B380. "Other premieres." *BMI, the many worlds of music* May 1971: 12.

A report of the premiere of *Apotheosis of this earth* [W56] at the Midwestern Music Conference, presented in a lecture-demonstration by the composer.

B381. Page, Tim. "Atlanta Symphony at Carnegie Hall." *New York Times,* 19 March, 1985, p.C12.

A review of the New York premiere of Husa's *Symphonic suite* [W48]. "There was much to admire--particularly the stark, proclamatory brass echoes that begin the work, the strength and concision of Mr. Husa's motifs, a composer's panoramic use of orchestral color."

B382. ----. "Recital: The Verdehr Trio presents music of the 80s." *New York Times,* 19 Dec., 1982, p.81.

A review of a concert by the Verdehr Trio, including a performance of Husa's *Sonata a tre* [W22]: " . . . a long and rhapsodic work that features taut energy and unrelenting central tension."

B383. Paine, Sylvia. *"Music for Prague* a tragic love song." *Sunday Forum* (Fargo-Moorhead, ND), 16 Nov., 1980, sect. B, p.1.

A report of a rehearsal, conducted by Husa, of the Fargo-Moorhead Symphony Orchestra, for a concert including a performance of Husa's *Music for Prague, 1968* [W41]. "Building solidly on a classical foundation, Husa has made the most of the contemporary freedom to experiment and innovate."

B384. Parsons, Arrand. "Music for Prague, 1968: Karel Husa." *Chicago Symphony*

Orchestra program notes, April 5-7, 1973: 9-11.

Notes accompanying a concert by the Chicago Symphony Orchestra, featuring a performance of Husa's *Music for Prague, 1968* [W41]. Includes a brief biography on the composer, and Husa's own comments on the composition.

B385. ----. "Music for Prague, 1968: Karel Husa." *Chicago Symphony Orchestra program notes,* Dec.11-16, 1986: 29-30.

Notes accompanying a concert by the Chicago Symphony Orchestra, featuring a performance of Husa's *Music for Prague, 1968* [W41]. The notes for the concert cited above were reprinted in this issue.

B386. Passy, Charles. "Intrigue in the Park." *Newsday* (New York), 3 Aug., 1988.

A review of the New York premiere of Husa's *Concerto,* for percussion and wind ensemble [W57]. "Though remarkably well-crafted, as evidenced by its tight three-movement construction and its brilliant and varied use of percussion, it also impresses on a purely visceral level, thanks to its impending sense of mystery."

B387. "People." *Society news : news from the Society for New Music* (Syracuse, NY) 5, no.1 (August 1989): 6.

Announcement of various awards, premieres and other performances Husa and his music had recently received.

B388. "People in music." *People in music* 57, no.9 (May 1986): 28-29.

Announcement that Ithaca College presented an honorary Doctor of Music degree to Husa during its 1986 commencement ceremonies. Includes brief biographical information, and lists of some awards, works and performances.

B389. Pion, S. "New York City Center." *Music journal* 29, no.3 (March 1971): 80.

A report on the performance of *Ontogeny,* presented by the American Ballet Theatre, choreographed by Dennis Nahat to the music of Husa's *String quartet,* no.3 [W16].

B390. Pitcher, W.J. "Land of opportunity right here in K-W." *Kitchener-Waterloo Record,* 2 May, 1964, p.9.

Announcement that Husa had been engaged to replace conductor Geoffrey Waddington for a concert, by members of the CBC and Toronto Symphony Orchestras, of music by Bach and Handel.

B391. ----. "Memorable program marks anniversary." *Kitchener-Waterloo Record,* 4 May, 1964.

A review of a concert by members of the CBC and Toronto Symphony Orchestras, conducted by Husa and featuring works of Handel and J.S. Bach. "Both choir and soloists, accompanied by the orchestra, expertly led by Mr. Husa, acquitted themselves with distinction. . . ."

B392. Plush, Vincent. "American composers down under." *24 hours* (Australian Broadcasting Association) 13, no.5 (June 1988): 10-11+.

An article about John Corigliano and Husa, accompanying the Chicago Symphony Orchestra on its tour of Australia. Includes brief biographical information, and discusses Husa's *Concerto,* for trumpet and orchestra [W51]. " . . . the Concerto appears to traverse conventional territory, but it also contains recollections of eminent Americans who visited Prague in Husa's youth--Woody Herman, Louis Armstrong, Duke Ellington and Count Basie."

B393. "Potpourri." *Instrumentalist* 23, no.1 (August 1968): 12.

A report of a concert by the Wind Ensemble of Cornell University, featuring three world premieres, including Husa's *Concerto,* for alto saxophone and band [W54a].

B394. "Potpourri." *Instrumentalist* 24, no.9 (April 1970): 8.

A report of Husa's month-long guest-conducting tour of Europe, highlighting performances of his works with the Czech Philharmonic for a recording of his *Symphony,* no.1 [W32], and the the Munich Philharmonic in the European premiere of his *Music for Prague, 1968* [W41].

B395. "Potpourri: Winning composition." *Instrumentalist* 38, no.9 (April 1984): 73.

A report that Husa's *Concerto,* for wind ensemble [W60] won the first Sudler International Wind Band Composition Competition. Includes background on the competition and the winning composition.

B396. Povich, Elaine S. "Karel Husa: Music 'of this earth'." *Cornell Daily Sun,* 3 May, 1973, p.9.

An interview with Karel Husa, who discusses his early life and education, and his career as a composer. "No composer lives from what he makes from his writing--one cannot live from what one has studied for 15 years, isn't that a paradox in life?"

B397. Prantl, Pavel. "Czech-American connections." *Singapore Symphony Orchestra news* 6, issue 1 (March 1987): 1-2.

The author calls this article "an appreciation in conjuction with the visit of guest conductor Professor Karel Husa." Prantl discusses the lives and music of Bohuslav Martinu and Husa. " . . . Husa still continues to contribute to the glory of the real musical superpower, the United States."

B398. "Preger and Husa share Boulanger award." *Musical America* 69, (July 1949): 29.

The announcement that judges Aaron Copland, Serge Koussevitsky, Walter Piston, Igor Stravinsky and Nadia Boulanger had chosen Leo Preger and Karel Husa to share the 1949 Lili Boulanger memorial Fund award.

B399. "Premieres." *BMI, the many worlds of music* July 1965: 18.

A report of the American Contemporary Music Project of Goucher College (Towson, MD), held in association with the Rockefeller Foundation and the Baltimore Symphony Orchestra, which presented the American premiere of Husa's *Symphony*, no. 1 [W32].

B400. "Premieres." *BMI, the many worlds of music* July 1966: 7.

A report on the spring concert of the Iota chapter of the Kappa Gamma Psi fraternity, which included the premiere of Husa's *Two preludes*, for woodwind trio [W15], as well as works by other composers.

B401. "Premieres." *BMI, the many worlds of music* Oct. 1966: 13.

A report of the American premiere of *Mosaïques* [W38], a feature of the May 7, 1966 concert: "American music in the University," by the Buffalo Philharmonic.

B402. "Premieres." *BMI, the many worlds of music* June 1968: 19.

A report of the world premiere of Husa's *Concerto*, for alto saxophone and concert band [W54a].

B403. "Premieres." *BMI, the many worlds of music* Jan. 1969: 15.

A report of the premiere of Husa's *String quartet*, no. 3 [W16], reviewed in the *Chicago Sun* by Robert C. March, who found a "genuinely imaginative quality" in the work.

B404. "Premieres." *BMI, the many worlds of music* May 1969: 10.

A report of the 1969 MENC Eastern Division Conference, including the world premiere of *Music for Prague, 1968* [W55], performed by the Ithaca College Concert Band, Kenneth Snapp, conducting.

B405. "Premieres." *BMI, the many worlds of music* May 1970: 17.

A report of the world premiere of the *Concerto*, for brass quintet and string orchestra [W40], including reviews from the *Buffalo Courier-Express*: "characterized by brilliant colors and rhythmic energy", and the *Buffalo Evening News*: "brilliant and stirring rhythmic complications and dramatic thrust."

B406. "Premieres." *BMI, the many worlds of music* Jan. 1971: 6.

A report of the American premiere of *Music for Prague, 1968* [W41] performed by the Baltimore Symphony Orchestra, Sergiu Comissiona conducting.

B407. "Premieres." *BMI, the many worlds of music* Summer 1971: 27.

A report of the world premiere of *Apotheosis of this earth* [W56] and the award of the Goldman Memorial Citation to Karel Husa. "Recipients of this citation were chosen because of their outstanding efforts and contributions to the development and improvement of concert bands and band music."

B408. "Premieres." *International musician* 69, no.8 (February 1971): 11.

An announcement of the American premiere of the orchestral version of Husa's *Music for Prague, 1968* [W41].   Also mentions some future performances of the work.

B409. "Premieres." *Music journal* 26, no.5 (May 1968): 44.

An announcement of the world premiere of Husa's *Concerto*, for alto saxophone and concert band [W54a].

B410. "Premieres." *Music journal* 27, no.4 (January 1969): 80.

An announcement of the world premiere of Husa's *String quartet*, no. 3 [W16].

B411. "Premieres." *Music journal* 28, no.4 (April 1970): 8.

An announcement of the world premiere of Husa's *Concerto*, for brass quintet and strings [W40].

B412. "Premieres." *Symphony news* 23, no.3 (1972): 30.

An announcement of the world premiere of Husa's *Two sonnets from Michelangelo* [W42].

B413. "Premieres." *Symphony news* 27, no.4 (1976): 45.

An announcement of the world premiere of Husa's *Monodrama* [W44].

B414. "Premieres." *Symphony magazine* 31, no.5 (1980): 40.

An announcement of the world premiere of Husa's *Pastoral*, for string orchestra [W45].

B415. "Premiers." *Music educators journal* 58, no.7 (March 1972): 118.

An announcement of the world premiere of Husa's *Concerto*, for percussion and wind ensemble [W57].

B416. "Premiers." *Music educators journal* 60, no.8 (April 1974): 125.

An announcement of the world premiere of Husa's *Sonata*, for violin and piano [W17].

B417. "Premiers." *Music educators journal* 61, no.8 (April 1975): 92.

An announcement of the world premiere of Husa's *Al fresco* [W59].

B418. "Premiers." *Music educators journal* 62, no.1 (September 1975): 96.

An announcement of the world premieres of Husa's *Al fresco* [W59] and *Steadfast tin soldier* [W43].

B419. "Premiers." *Music educators journal* 62, no.8 (April 1976): 14.

An announcement of the world premiere of Husa's *Sonata*, no.2, for piano [W5].

B420. "Premiers." *Music educators journal* 63, no.1 (September 1976): 22.

An announcement of the world premiere of Husa's *Monodrama* [W44].

B421. "Premiers." *Music educators journal* 63, no.9 (May 1977): 66-67.

An announcement of the world premiere of Husa's *An American Te Deum* [W65a].

B422. "Premiers." *Music educators journal* 64, no.7 (March 1978): 114.

An announcement of the world premiere of Husa's *Landscapes*, for brass quintet [W18].

B423. "Premiers." *Music educators journal* 67, no.4 (December 1980): 21.

An announcement of the world premieres of Husa's *Pastoral*, for string orchestra [W45], *Three dance sketches*, for percussion quartet [W19], and *Intradas and interludes*, for seven trumpets and percussion [W20].

B424. Price, Rick. "Husa's piano offerings worthy of a recording." *Leader* (Corning, NY), 20 Oct., 1973, p.5.

A review of a performance of Husa's keyboard music: *Sonatina* [W1], *Sonata no.1* [W2], *Elegie* [W4], and *Eight Czech duets* [W3]. " . . . the composer seems up to his usually [sic] sensible standard, assimilating the pronounced, often stylized elements of earlier musicians and blending them to form another style that is distinctly his own."

B425. ----. "Music of composer Karel Husa stays in tune with the times." *Leader* (Corning, NY), 29 Oct., 1973, p.2.

An interview with Husa, conducting a master class for a day-long piano workshop. "Today's music is just attempting to keep up with society, and it must change faster now than it did in the past because society is shifting rapidly. Music must relate to the present."

B426. ----. "Practice still key to success: Husa." *Leader* (Corning, NY), 30 Oct.,

1973, p.5.

A report of a master class conducted by Husa, part of a day-long piano workshop. "Composers are in professional competition, and the tendency is for them to write more and more difficult things so their fellow writers can't beat them on technique. There are comparatively few composers able to write pieces simple enough for children to play without winding up with music that is trite."

B427. Price, Theodore. "Husa's passion." *Rochester Democrat and Chronicle*, 19 Oct., 1972.

Interview with Husa, prior to conducting the Eastman Wind Ensemble performing his *Concerto*, for percussion and wind ensemble [W57]. "Music for me is not just excitement, not just enchantment--. . . it's a passion for me. And I decided to become a musician just for that feeling of passion."

B428. ----. "Lackluster Ives' Fourth in Washington." *Rochester Democrat and Chronicle*, 7 Sept., 1972, p.4C.

A review of a concert by the Fine Arts Quartet, including Husa's *String quartet*, no.3 [W16]. "It is one of the few post-war works in any medium which fully exploits string sonorities without stooping to cliches."

B429. ----. "Primeval essence." *Rochester Democrat and Chronicle*, 21 Oct., 1972.

A review of a concert including Husa's *Concerto*, for percussion and wind ensemble [W57], performed by the Eastman Wind Ensemble. "It is 18 minutes of intense, at times feverish, but clearly spelled out musical hyperactivity."

B430. Pryor, Allan. "Chamber group cites composer." *Syracuse Herald-Journal*, 24 April, 1971, p.3.

A review of a "Friends of chamber music" concert honoring Husa, and including his *Serenade*, for woodwind quintet and string orchestra [W39] and *Poem*, for viola and chamber orchestra [W36]. "Most of his works . . . are not only well-constructed and well-orchestrated; they are interesting and individual, and they project strong personality."

B431. "The Pulitzer Prize." *BMI, the many worlds of music* Summer 1969: 42.

A report of Husa's 1969 Pulitzer Prize award for music. Includes some biographical information, and quotes from Elliott W. Galkin's article "A deserving music Pulitzer Prize winner" [SEE B168]. "With the award to

Husa . . . recognition has been accorded a musician whose orientation is exquisitely classical and whose language, while original and searching for new means of self expression, can be understood as belonging to the mainstream of compositional practices during the first half of this century."

B432. "Pulitzer Prize winner will lecture, conduct." *Cleveland Plain-Dealer*, 21 May, 1976, sect.6, p.5.

A report that Husa would be in residence at Kent State University, lecturing on contemporary music and conducting the Ohio premiere of his *An American Te Deum* [W65a].

B433. "The Pulitzer prizes (some winners in music)." *BMI, the many worlds of music* 2 (1974): 26.

Photographs and brief acknowledgement of the works of the Pulitzer Prize winners in music, including Karel Husa, for his *String quartet*, no.3 [W16]. "Working from an essentially classical position, he compounds elements of the past and present, using his own distinctly individual recipe."

B434. "A Pulitzer winner by Karel Husa." *Saturday review* 54, no.44 (Oct.30, 1971): 72.

A review of the Everest recording [D28] of Husa's *String quartets*, nos.2 and 3 [W12 & W16]. " . . . the jury can take pride in having selected a work of unquestionable competence, professionalism, and clear-cut credentials. . . . The Fine Arts ensemble . . . plays the work like men possessed . . ."

B435. Putnam, Thomas. "Czechs honored by Philharmonic." *Buffalo Courier-Express*, 17 Feb., 1970, p.5.

A review of a concert by the Buffalo Philharmonic Orchestra, including the world premiere of Husa's *Concerto*, for brass quintet and string orchestra [W40]. " . . . characterized by brilliant colors and rythmic energy. . . . There is lyricism, too. . . . Husa builds tension which is resolved in a satisfying manner."

B436. ----. "Janacek Mass offered." *Buffalo Courier Express*, 8 April, 1968, p.22.

Review of a performance of Janáček's *Glagolitic Mass* by the Buffalo Philharmonic, conducted by Karel Husa, in a program including his *Symphony*, no.1 [W32]. "Husa's *Symphony* is a big chunk of music. It has a grand sense of dramatic tension, and the orchestra sounds good. . . . Husa keeps the air tense and electric, but he never fails to give a full resolution."

B437. Rackemann, Adelaide C. "Music in review: Baltimore Symphony presents two world premieres at Lyric." *Baltimore Evening Sun*, 8 Jan., 1964.

A review of a concert by the Baltimore Symphony Orchestra, including the world premiere performance of Husa's *Serenade*, for woodwind quintet with xylophone, harp and strings [W39]. " . . . a refreshing piece of music, easy to listen to, although obviously modern . . . It is an imaginative, unusual work, played superbly by both the orchestra and the excellent quintet."

B438. Raeburn, Andrew H. "Mosaïques pour orchestre." *Boston Symphony Orchestra program notes*, April 19, 1968: 1436-1442.

Notes to accompany a concert by the Boston Symphony Orchestra, including a performance of Husa's *Mosaïques* [W38]. Includes brief biographical information and background on the work performed, and a note provided by Husa. "Perhaps the first *Mosaïque* may remind one of the 'city of 100 towers'; the second and third of winter and spring in Prague. The fourth could be the picture of a tragedy, and the fifth, the succeeding moment of quiet."

B439. Ram, Jane. "Husa triumph." *South China Morning Post*, 16 Jan., 1981.

A review of a concert by the Hong Kong Philharmonic, featuring Husa's *Music for Prague, 1968* [W41]. "This powerful and triumphant work alone made the evening thoroughly worthwhile."

B440. ----. "Talking about good music . . . " *South China Morning Post*, 21 Jan., 1981.

A review of a Hong Kong Philharmonic family concert, conducted by Husa, and including the finale from his *Music for Prague, 1968* [W41], with works by Beethoven, Mozart and Smetana. "When played like it [Smetana's *Die Moldau*] was on Sunday, the pictorial writing never fails to thrill. . . . The finale from Mr. Husa's *Music for Prague, 1968* formed an unforgettable end to the afternoon."

B441. Ramey, Philip. "Notes on the program: Concerto for orchestra." *New York Philharmonic program notes*, Sept.25-30, 1986.

Notes accompanying the world premiere of Husa's *Concerto*, for orchestra [W49]. Includes biographical data, and quotes from the composer on his *Concerto*: "Above all, my Concerto for Orchestra . . . concentrates on virtuosic orchestral playing, featuring not only soloists, but also various sections and the entire ensemble as well."

B442. ----. "Notes on the program: "Music for Prague, 1968" for orchestra." *Stagebill* (New York Philharmonic) 26, no.9 (May 1989): 16.

Notes accompanying a performance of Husa's *Music for Prague, 1968* [W41]. Includes biographical information and the composer's commentary.

B443. Raney, Carolyn. "The assesors assessed." *Music: The A.G.O. and R.C.C.O. magazine* 6, Issue 12 (December 1972): 23-25.

A report of the 1972 convention of the Music Critics Association, including a panel of composers and conductors discussing the present direction of contemporary music. "Karel Husa appeared to be the neo-humanist on the panel. He approaches his writing with a view towards supplying a need, whether he is commissioned to write a string quartet or an opera."

B444. Rauzi, Robin. "USC Symphony debuts concerto: Husa work features cello solo by Professor Harrell." *Daily Trojan* (University of Southern California) 108, no.36 (March 7, 1989): 1.

A report of the world premiere of Husa's *Concerto*, for violoncello and orchestra [W52]. Includes brief biographical information and a background of the work.

B445. "Readers write." *Accent on music* 7, no.1 (September/ October 1981): 12.

A letter from a reader, relating the experience of playing under Husa's baton. "Every member of the band put all they had into playing his work in a tribute to an exceptionally talented man who had composed a work of such importance."

B446. Rehert, Isaac. "Teacher, composer Husa in concert at Peabody." *Baltimore Sun*, 2 Oct., 1979, p.B6.

Interview with Husa, visiting instructor at the Peabody Institute. Asked if he thought of himself as a romantic, he replied: "If by romantic you mean an artist who fancies himself some special kind of human being, no. But if a romantic means somebody who feels as well as thinks, who responds to the world around him, who when he writes or performs gets at least some of his inspiration from what is happening in the world, then, yes, I am a romantic."

B447. Reinthaler, Joan. "Husa's 'Te Deum': focus on majesty." *Washington Post*, 11 May, 1978, p.C4.

A review of a performance of Husa's *An American Te Deum* [W65b] at the

Inter-American Music Festival, conducted by Husa. "... an interesting and effective piece of music, and one that would be good to hear again."

B448. "Reports from member organizations (Broadcast Music, Inc.)." *National Music Council bulletin,* 37, no.2 (Spring 1978): 21.

A report on some of Husa's activities during 1977, including conducting performances of his *Music for Prague, 1968* [W55] and *Concerto,* for percussion and wind ensemble [W57].

B449. Rexroat, Dee Ann. "Czech-American writes protest music for symphonies." *Cedar Rapids Gazette,* 6 May, 1988, p.3C.

A pre-performance interview with Husa, who discusses his *Music for Prague, 1968* [W41] and calls it "a statement for freedom."

B450. Rivers, Kate. "The Marine Band." *Washington Post,* 17 April, 1984, p.D2.

A review of a concert by the United States Marine Band, including the Washington premiere of Husa's *Concerto,* for wind ensemble [W60]. " . . . the work exploits thrilling rhythmic patterns . . . and quarter-tones. . . . All three movements reveal Husa's characteristically brilliant orchestrations."

B451. ----. "Thomas Oboe Lee wins Friedham award." *Washington Post,* 10 Oct., 1983, p.D13.

An announcement of the Kennedy Center's Friedham awards for 1983. Husa's *Recollections* [W23] received third prize: " . . . a work that explores the contrasting sonorities created by combining the piano and five winds in various ways."

B452. Robinson, Ray E. "Curzon, Husa share spotlight with Adler." *Baltimore Evening Sun,* 25 Nov., 1965.

A review of a concert by the Baltimore Symphony Orchestra, including a performance of Husa's *Symphony,* no.1 [W32]. " . . . a rather enigmatic work, using a large Nineteenth Century orchestra in a Twentieth Century idiom. . . . A well-written work, showing the labor of a master craftsman in the art of orchestration and composition."

B453. Rockwell, John. "Music: new works in tribute to science." *New York Times,* 31 Oct., 1987, p.10.

A review of the world premiere of Husa's *Concerto,* for organ and orchestra

[W50] at the Cleveland Institute of Music: " . . . this 22-minute score . . . sweeps along with a power and intensity that recalls Janacek."

B454. ----. "Concert: Tanglewood goes contemporary." *New York Times*, 3 Aug., 1981, p.C13.

A review of a concert at Tanglewood, including a performance of Husa's *Two Preludes* [W15]: "The Husa . . . seemed ernest, well crafted, honorably affecting and yet not really very strong or striking."

B455. Rogers, Rick. "Pulitzer-winning composer to speak at OU." *Daily Oklahoman*, 23 Feb., 1989, p.11.

An interview with Husa, whose music was the focus of a minifestival of contemporary music at the University of Oklahoma. Husa comments: "I believe that music really expresses what you see around you, almost like writing a chronicle of our own times."

B456. Rosenthal, Laurence. "*Sonate für Klavier, op. 11.*" *Notes* 10 (June 1953): 495.

A review of Husa's *Piano sonata*, op.11 [W2]. "The three movements of this powerfully wrought structure are obviously the work of a composer who posesses very considerable grasp and scope, and a searching ear. . . . This feels like the work of a young man, and as such it is an impressive performance."

B457. Ross, Marnie. "Eastern Philharmonic gives Husa brilliant, fiery best." *Greensboro Daily News*, 15 July, 1973, p.A14.

A review of a concert by the Eastern Philharmonic Orchestra, conducted by Husa and including his *Fresque* [W29b] and *Two sonnets by Michelangelo* [W42]. "All . . . are powerful works, and show that Husa is a genius at working with orchestral color, or timbres."

B458. Roth, Henry. "World of music: USC premiere." *B'nai B'rith Messenger*, 10 March, 1989.

A review of the world premiere of Husa's *Concerto*, for violoncello and orchestra [W52]. "Abrasive in mood, dense in orchestral sonorities, eclectic in harmonic device and fiercely individual in character, it demands the skills of a big-scaled player like Harrell."

B459. Rothbart, Peter. "CCO serves up a rich and varied program." *Ithaca Journal*, 9 Nov., 1981.

A review of a concert by the Cayuga Chamber Orchestra, conducted by Husa and featuring a performance of his *Divertimento*, for string orchestra [W30]. "The *Divertimento's* mercurial mood changes presented some serious technical challenges for the ensemble. . . . "

B460. ----. "A posher Tashi." *Ithaca Journal*, 11 Feb., 1982.

A review of a concert by Tashi, featuring works by Mozart, Weber, Bill Douglas, and Husa's *Evocations de Slovaquie* [W11a]. "Their performance . . . captured the old Tashi magic, revelling in Husa's Slavic folk melodies, both real and imaginary."

B461. Routte, Eneid. "Karel Husa : a composer of 'Manifests' for freedom." *San Juan Star/Portfolio* (Puerto Rico), 9 Feb., 1978, sect.P, p.1-2.

An interview with Karel Husa, in San Juan to conduct the Puerto Rico Symphony Orchestra in performances including his *Music for Prague, 1968* [W41]. The composer discusses his life, some recent compositions, and winning the Pulitzer Prize.

B462. Roy, Klaus. "*Music for Prague, 1968.*" *Cleveland Orchestra program notes*, Feb.26-27, 1971: 622-25.

Notes to accompany a concert by the Cleveland Orchestra, including a performance of Husa's *Music for Prague, 1968* [W41]. Includes Husa's own comments on the work.

B463. ----. "*Music for Prague, 1968.*" *Cleveland Orchestra program notes*, April 9-11, 1987: 31-39.

Notes to accompany a concert by the Cleveland Orchestra, including a performance of Husa's *Music for Prague, 1968* [W41]. Includes biographical information and a brief history of the composition and its performance.

B464. Ryker, Harrison. "Fine music." *Hong Kong Standard*, 11 Jan., 1981.

A review of a concert by the Hong Kong Philharmonic, conducted by Husa, including Haydn's *Symphony*, no.104 and Husa's *Music for Prague, 1968* [W41]. "He and the orchestra concluded their concert with a white-hot reading of it, which drew an enthusiastic demonstration from both the orchesta and the assembled audience."

B465. Sabin, Robert. "New music reviews: three piano sonatas in contrasting styles." *Musical America* 73, (September 1953): 20.

A review of piano sonatas by Halsey Stevens, Karel Husa [W2] and Volfgangs Darzins.

B466. Sadler, Graham. *"Les ballets des Muses* / J.B. Lully, ed. by Karel Husa." *Early music* 8, no.3 (1980): 397.

A review of Husa's editions of Lully's *Les ballets des Muses* [WA3]. " . . . the present edition of the hitherto unpublished *Ballets des Muses* can be given only the most lukewarm of welcomes."

B467. Sagmaster, Joseph. "Karel Husa: Symphony, no. 1." *Cincinnati Symphony Orchestra program notes*, April 26, 1968: 841-847.

Program notes accompanying a performance of Husa's *Symphony*, no.1 [W32] by the Cincinnati Symphony Orchestra. Very brief background information is provided, and comments by the composer are included.

B468. Salisbury, Wilma. "Creativity warmly received." *Cleveland Plain Dealer*, 30 Oct., 1987, p.11.

A review of the world premiere of Husa's *Concerto*, for organ and orchestra [W50] by the Cleveland Institute of Music Chamber Orchestra, with Karel Paukert, organist. "Like all of Husa's music, the concerto is crafted with assurance and expressed with honesty. . . . The piece received a stunning performance from Paukert, Husa and the CIM Chamber Orchestra."

B469. Salva, Tadeas. "Americké vízum pre slovensku hudbú? [American vision for Slovak music?]" *Nove slovo*, 8 Dec., 1988.

An interview with Slovakian composer Tadeas Salva, who speaks of various influences on his music. Of Husa, Salva says: "His music is original, he respects all innovations of the twentieth century, yet did not slide into the 'American coat,' but his compositional expression is exclusively personal. Here is an artist of a world format and we could learn much here from the quality of his creation." [translated from the Czech]

B470. Sanders, Forrest. "Music: Cornell University Chorus, Orchestra." *Ithaca Journal*, 25 Nov., 1957.

A review of a performance of Cherubini's *Requiem* and Mozart's *Funeral ode*, conducted by Husa. "When a conductor has a thorough knowledge of a score, a well-thought plan of presentation, a memory which encompasses every entrance, cue and dynamic marking, and a baton technic [sic] that is exact, clean cut, yet unobtrusive, it is a wonderful thing to watch him direct sans score."

B471. Saya, Virginia Montgomery. "Hungarian-born cellist gives stellar CSO debut." *Cincinnati Enquirer*, 24 Oct., 1987, p.C-6.

A review of a concert by the Cincinnati Symphony Orchestra, under the direction of David Loebel, including Husa's *Music for Prague, 1968* [W41]. "Loebel . . . has fine artistic instincts and the subtle podium technique to make his intentions known. This was most apparent in . . . Husa's work, . . . one of the few pieces of 'new' music programmed by the CSO in recent years that has brought much of the Music Hall audience to its feet."

B472. Schneider, John. "New work by Husa 'powerful'." *Atlanta Journal*, 19 March, 1976, p.18-A.

A review of a concert by the Atlanta Symphony Orchestra, including a performance of Husa's *Apotheosis of this earth* [W64]. "Husa succeeds in projecting his dour message with gripping force."

B473. Schneider, June. "Atlanta Symphony : Husa *Symphonic suite*." *High fidelity/Musical America* 35, no.2 (February 1985): MA22.

A review of a performance by the Atlanta Symphony of Husa's *Symphonic suite* [W48]. "Husa's powerfully communicative style is well-represented throughout."

B474. ----. "Atlanta Virtuosi : piano quartets by Husa, Schuller, Schwartz [premieres]." *High fidelity/Musical America* 34 (November, 1984): MA24.

A review of the premieres of three works commissioned for the Atlanta Virtuosi: piano quartets by Husa, Gunther Schuller and Elliot Schwartz. "The works . . . constitute a significant contribution to the piano quartet literature. . . . Husa's *Variations* [W24] is a particularly interesting and evocative study in sonority and texture. . . . "

B475. ----. "Atlanta Virtuosi makes history." *Atlanta Constitution*, 21 May, 1984, p.3C.

A review of the world premiere of Husa's *Variations* [W24]. " . . . a fascinating cobweb of sound, at times extremely gentle, but with great tension, and with an interesting inner rhythmic compulsion at other times."

B476. Schuh, Willi. "Das 34. Weltmusikfest in Koln." *Schweizerische Musikzeitung* 100, no.5 (1960): 314.

An article (in German) on the 34th Weltmusikfest in Cologne, including the world premiere of Husa's *Poem*, for viola and chamber orchestra [W36].

Schuh singled out the *Poem* as deserving of special notice.

B477. Sciannameo, Franco. "Karel Husa--Sonata a Tre for violin, B flat clarinet and piano." *Violexchange* 4, no.1 (1989): 22.

A review of Husa's *Sonata a tre* [W22]. "The piece is no recreational ensemble reading; it is a work intensely complex in which hundreds of sonic possibilities are employed in an individual and collective virtuosic fashion."

B478. Scott, Lee. "Karel Husa: Composer's career builds to a crescendo." *Ithaca Journal*, 11 May, 1984, p.9.

In this article, Husa discusses the inspiration for his composition *The Trojan women* [W46a] and his career as a composer and educator. "I love teaching. A composer who teaches is very fortunate. He has the resources of the university where he works and he continues to learn along with his students. I never get old in musical ideas. The kids keep me in the mainstream."

B479. Seligmann, Raphael. "His muse's voice: Mozart by the CCO." *Ithaca Times*, 17-23 Sept., 1981.

A review of a concert by the Cayuga Chamber Orchestra, conducted by Husa. "Husa elicited from his players and singers moments of angular precision and sinuous lyricism and the whole range of qualities in between."

B480. ----. "The Husa sweep cleans up." *Ithaca Times*, 11-17 Feb., 1982.

A review of a concert by the Cayuga Chamber Orchestra, conducted by Husa. "Husa's style enlivens music of all eras."

B481. ----. "Terrestrial 'Messiah'." *Ithaca Times*, 17-22 Dec., 1981: 26+.

A review of a performance of Handel's *Messiah*, conducted by Husa. "It was . . . style that made last Sunday's *Messiah* by the Cayuga Chamber Orchestra and the Cornell Chorale a successful performance, and it was . . . problems of technique which kept it from being a memorable one."

B482. Shulgold, Marc. "Karel Husa : putting his convictions to music." *Los Angeles Times*, 1 March, 1986, sect.V, p.1+.

An interview with Husa, who discusses his life and the various cultural influences on his work, especially *Music for Prague, 1968* [W41], which he conducted with the Orange County Pacific Symphony Orchestra. "I consider myself an international composer. . . . I have been touched by several cultures. And that *must* show in my music."

B483. Simmons, Harwood. "Books and music for review." *School music news,* April 1970.

A list of new educational recordings by the Cornell University Wind Ensemble, including recordings [D5] of Husa's *Music for Prague, 1968* [W55]: ". . . an emotional outpouring in which the composer portrays the tragic events which took place in his native city," and, *Concerto,* for alto saxophone and concert band [W54a]: "A masterpiece in every respect."

B484. Simmons, Walter. "Husa: Sonata for violin and piano." *Fanfare* 2, no.4 (March/April, 1979): 67-68.

A review of a recording [D26] of Husa's *Sonata,* for violin and piano [W17]. "Husa exploits fully the rhetoric of textural masses and sound shapes divorced from traditional melody, tonality and meter, yet retains a clarity of thematic contour and never abandons an immediate theatrical impact."

B485. Simpson, Mitch. "Pulitzer Prize winner is Music Festival guest." *Greensboro Daily News,* 19 July, 1971.

An interview with Husa, guest composer/conductor for the Eastern Music Festival. Husa discusses his education in Prague and Paris, and some of his recent compositions. "I have been writing more absolute, pure music in the past, but during the last 2 or 3 years, I feel that I want to write things related to the present stage."

B486. Skei, Allen B. "Karel Husa: String quartet no.3." *Notes,* 29, no.3 (March, 1973): 556.

A review of Husa's *String quartet,* no.3 [W16]. "Karel Husa's Third String Quartet . . . makes at its outset and at the beginning of each succeeding movement musical promises that seek but never find fulfillment."

B487. Slein, Judy. "Emotion, power mark piano works of Cornell composer." *Ithaca Journal,* 13 Nov., 1978.

A review of a concert featuring Husa's piano music, performed by Mary Ann Covert. " . . . the composer is obviously concerned not only for his listener's intellectual satisfaction, but for his emotional satisfaction as well."

B488. ----. "Husa's 'Te Deum' is perfectly performed." *Ithaca Journal*, 2 May, 1979, p.6.

A review of a performance of Husa's *An American Te Deum* [W65a] by the Cornell University Chorus and Glee Club and the Eastman Wind Ensemble. "It is endlessly varied and intriguing and yet, however much variety there is, it all contributes to a powerful, cohesive whole."

B489. Sobelman, Nina. "Berlioz 'Requiem,' Bailey Hall." *Ithaca Journal*, 12 Dec., 1966.

A review of a performance of Berlioz' *Requiem*, by the Cornell University Glee Club and Chorus, Symphony Orchestra and Brass Ensemble. "This musical event was made what it was by the intelligent conducting of Mr. Husa."

B490. ----. "Buffalo Philharmonic at Bailey Hall." *Ithaca Journal*, 11 April, 1968, p.12.

Review of a performance by the Buffalo Philharmonic, conducted by Husa, and including a performance of his *Symphony*, no.1 [W32]. "The *Symphony* . . . and the Janacek *Slavonic Mass* together made a very passionate combination. Both works express a strong Czech feeling and background, both stylistically to some degree and, to a greater degree, in subtler emotional ways. Under Mr. Husa's dynamic direction both works took shape and were excitingly performed."

B491. ----. "Clay concert: Bailey Hall." *Ithaca Journal*, 11 May, 1966.

A review of the American premiere of Husa's *Mosaïques* [W38]. ". . . the music as interpreted by the composer has an organic continuity that makes it accessible even to the new listener."

B492. ----. "Composer's panel; Chamber orchestra." *Ithaca Journal*, 18 Nov., 1968.

A review of a concert by the Cornell Chamber Orchestra, which included a performance of Husa's *Poem*, for viola and chamber orchestra [W36]. "Mr. Husa conducts with impeccable taste. . . . He is able to balance any instrumental texture."

B493. ----. "Cornell Symphony." *Ithaca Journal*, 22 April, 1968.

A review of a concert by the Cornell Orchestra, featuring works by Roussel, Dukas, Kay, Mozart and Schumann, and conducted by Husa. "Yesterday's performance was marked by its masculine strength and its intelligence; it has been a long time since this symphony was so engrossing."

B494. ----. "Music: Chamber Orchestra, Chorus at Cornell." *Ithaca Journal*, 8 March, 1967.

A review of a concert by the Cornell Chamber Orchestra with the Cornell Chamber Chorus and Cornell Chorus, conducted by Husa, and including a performance of Michel Delalande's motet *Cantate Domino*, arr. by Husa [WA4]. "The performance of the motet was most effective. It showed . . . that Mr. Husa--a truly superior musician--is capable of carrying off quite ambitious and challenging projects, with great success."

B495. ----. "Music: Cornell Orchestra at Bailey Hall." *Ithaca Journal*, 17 April, 1967.

A review of a performance by the Cornell Orchestra, featuring works by Honegger, Persichetti, Gershwin and Brahms and conducted by Husa. "One would have to commend Mr. Husa simply for making this venture at all; but he succeeded in doing infinitely more. . . . As this entire program amply demonstrated, Mr. Husa is a conductor of unfailing taste and musicianship."

B496. ----. "Music Review: Composer's Forum; Philharmonic concert." *Ithaca Journal*, 15 April, 1968, p.9.

A report of a composer's forum featuring Elliott Carter, Karel Husa and Alan Hovhaness. Each panelist discussed the evolution of his musical style, commented on the relationship between his music and the audience, and on the present state of music. Part 2 of the review was of a performance of the Buffalo Philharmonic Orchestra, conducted by Karel Husa, and featuring works by Hovhaness, Ginastera, Carter and Schuman.

B497. ----. "New music: more listeners merited." *Ithaca Journal*, 10 April, 1968.

An interview with Husa, who discusses modern music, the critic and the audience. "We are definitely going through a period of searching and looking; this is not our fault, . . . but the result of our times and Time. . . . Universities are in a critically important niche . . . to provide concert opportunities for both students and university public to hear new music."

B498. Southgate, Harvey. "New music colors UN concert." *Rochester Chronicle*, 23 Oct., 1969.

A review of the 17th annual United Nations concert at Eastman Theater. The performance by the Eastman Wind Ensemble included Husa's *Music for Prague, 1968* [W55]. "With virtually no melodic appeal, the work does have an overall emotional effect, its dissonances possibly indicative of the Prague of today, its strangely mixed instrumental voices possibly prophetic of the music of tomorrow."

B499. "Special commissions." *Pan pipes* 67, no.2 (January 1975): 34.

An announcement that the Chamber Music Society of Lincoln Center commissioned Husa for his composition *Sonata*, for violin and piano [W17].

B500. Speer, Danny. "CCO's 'King David' an artistic success." *Ithaca Times*, 22-28 March, 1984.

A review of a performance by the Cayuga Chamber Orchestra, featuring Honegger's *King David*, conducted by Husa. "The music was well prepared and a total success from an artistic point of view."

B501. ----. "Husa's star shines at CCO evening." *Ithaca Times*, 24 Feb.-2 March, 1983.

A review of a concert by the Cayuga Chamber Orchestra, including a performance of Husa's *Portrait*, for string orchestra [W33] and conducted by Husa. "Husa's music requires an intellectual effort from the listener. Its harmonic structures are far from easily digested, but it is emotionally charged, and at times hauntingly beautiful."

B502. Staff, Charles. "ISO audience enthralled by modern 'Prague'." *Indianapolis News*, 22 Oct., 1982, p.22.

A review of a performance of *Music for Prague, 1968* [W41] by the Indianapolis Symphony Orchestra, under the direction of John Nelson. "For a change, a modern piece of music proved the most exciting event on an Indianapolis Symphony Orchestra concert."

B503. Stehman, Jacques. "Les concerts: Pia Sebastiani et Karel Husa." *Le Soir* (Brussels), 14 Feb., 1967.

A review of a concert by the Belgium Radio and Television Orchestra, conducted by Husa, and including a performance of his *Symphony*, no.1 [W32]. "Sa *Symphonie*, no.1, incontestablement interéssante, dramatique, personnelle, serait plus captivante encore si elle était abregée et amputée de quelques stridences." [His *Symphony*, no.1, uncontestably interesting, dramatic, personal, would be even more captivating if certain stridencies were abridged and even lopped off.]

B504. Steinberg, Michael. "Husa's composition provides Symphony concert treat." *Boston Globe*, 20 April, 1968.

A review of a performance by the Boston Symphony Orchestra of Husa's *Mosaïques* [W38], conducted by Eric Leinsdorf. "It is interesting and consistently worked, and it is scored with unostentatious, ungimmicky originality, beauty and effectiveness."

B505. Stith, G. "A survey of ambiguous wind articulations." *Instrumentalist* 32, no.3 (March 1978): 30-32.

A report of a survey of twenty distinguished American composers, including Husa, asking for definitions of four different, but also ambiguous, articulations. In his additional comments, Husa states: "The modern composers were aware of some of the inadequacies of the notation, and tried to be as precise as possible."

B506. Strini, Tom. "Command." *Milwaukee Journal Magazine*, Nov.20, 1988: 11.

A study of maestro Zdenek Macal, conductor of the Milwaukee Symphony Orchestra, as he rehearses Husa's *Music for Prague, 1968* [W41].

B507. Strongin, Theodore. "Musicians open Cornell festival: Lincoln Center is scene of centennial concert." *New York Times*, 11 March, 1965, p.38.

A review of a performance of Beethoven's *Missa Solemnis* by the Cornell Symphony Orchestra, Chorus and Glee Club, conducted by Husa. "Mr. Husa's pacing was just right, his sense of emphasis strong and he drew from his forces phrasing and nuance on a professional level without dimming amateur fervor."

B508. Stuckenschmidt, H.H. "Expressionistic tendencies dominant in Donaueschingen festival premieres." *Musical America* 73 (December 1, 1953): 30.

A report on the Donaueschingen Festival premieres, including Karel Husa's *Portrait*, for string orchestra [W33]: ". . . a piece of vigorous, deeply emotional Czech music, in the vein of Josef Suk."

B509. Stucky, Steve. "Composers Quartet, CU Chamber series." *Ithaca Journal*, 6 Dec., 1971.

Review of a concert by the Composers String Quartet, which included a performance of Husa's *String quartet*, no.2 [W12]. "It is a brilliant, colorful piece, full of virtuoso writing. . . . "

B510. Sturm, George. "Encounters: Karel Husa." *MadAmina!* 1, no.2 (Spring, 1981): 7-9.

A biographical article on Karel Husa, highlighting his early studies with Nadia Boulanger and the composition of his best-known works, including *Music for Prague, 1968* [W41].

B511. ----. "A Husa chronicle." *MadAmina!* 4, no.2 (Fall 1983): 11.

A report of Husa's recent activities, including performances of *Recollections*, for woodwind quintet and piano [W23], the world premieres of his *Concerto*, for wind ensemble [W60], *Cantata*, for men's chorus and brass quintet [W68], and *Reflections* (Symphony no.2) [W47], as well as various performances of his *Sonata a tre* [W22].

B512. ----. "Husa travels with two new works." *MadAminA!* 10, no.1 (Spring, 1989): 7.

An outline of Husa's travel schedule for early 1989, including the Australian tour of the Chicago Symphony Orchestra and the world premiere of his *Concerto*, for violoncello and orchestra [W52].

B513. ----. "Husa's *Trojan women* triumphs in Louisville." *MadAminA!* 2, no.2 (Fall 1981): 4.

A report of the world premiere of the ballet *The Trojan women*, with music composed by Husa [W46a]. Includes excerpts from local reviews.

B514. ----. "Karel Husa: new composition, recordings, publications." *MadAminA!* 3, no.2 (Fall 1983): 7.

A report of three Husa world premieres [W67, W22, W23], the debut of two recordings [D30, D10], and the publication of new Husa scores [W58a, W45, W19, W65c, W66, W65a].

B515. ----.   "Karel Husa: recent performances, commission, recordings." *MadAminA!* 10, no.2 (Fall 1989): 9-10.

A report of performances of *Music for Prague, 1968* [W41] and *Sonata a tre* [W22], the issuance of *Music for Prague, 1968* on compact disc [D21] and the publication of the score to *Smetana fanfare* [W61]. Also announces the world premiere of *Concerto*, for violoncello and orchestra [W52], and the postponement of the world premiere of *String quartet, no.4* [W26].

B516. ----. "Karel Husa at 65." *MadAminA!* 7 no.2 (Fall, 1986): 10.

An enumeration of the many concerts planned in celebration of Husa's 65th birthday, including the Boston 65th Birthday Celebration of Husa.

B517. ----. "Karel Husa plans busy 60th year." *MadAminA!* 1, no.1 (Fall, 1980): 7.

A report of Husa's 1980 schedule of performances, including summer appearances at the Interlochen Music Festival, the Bowdoin Summer Festival, UCLA, Cal State (Northridge) and the Universities of Oklahoma and Wisconsin.

B518. ----. "Sudler Prize, Sousa Medal awarded to Husa." *MadAminA!* 5, no.2 (Fall 1984): 8-9.

A report that Husa's *Concerto*, for wind ensemble [W60] won the first biennial Sudler International Wind Band Composition competition, including the Medal of the Sousa Order of Merit. Also mentions the choreographing of his *String quartet*, no.3 [W16], the forthcoming world premiere of his *Symphonic suite* [W48] and performances of his *Variations*, for piano quartet [W24].

B519. ----. "Two new Husa concertos introduced." *MadAminA!* 9, no.1 (Spring 1988): 7.

A report of the world premieres of Husa's *Concerto*, for organ and orchestra [W50] and *Concerto*, for trumpet and orchestra [W51].

B520. ----. "The uplifting and exhilarating ways of Karel Husa." *MadAminA!* 6, no.1 (Spring 1985): 10-11.

A report of the world premiere of Husa's *Symphonic suite* [W48], and subsequent performances of the work by the Atlanta Symphony. Also mentions performances of *Variations*, for piano quartet [W24] and *The Trojan women* [W46a].

B521. Subramaniam, Vinod. "Interesting & bizarre." *Cornell Daily Sun*, 7 March, 1988.

A review of a performance of Husa's *Frammenti*, for organ [W6]. "The contrasting pace of the movements jolted the listener from unsuspecting complacency and made one sit up and notice the music."

B522. "Symposium: The career labyrinth." *Executive* (Graduate School of Business and Public Administration, Cornell University) 2, no.2 (Winter 1976): 17.

Husa briefly discusses career requirements for a successful modern composer. "It is important, then, that the composer be able to interpret his own work, that he master an instrument or learn to conduct, and that he learn to speak and analyze his work before an audience."

B523. "Syracuse Symphony to offer work by Cornell U. composer." *Syracuse Post-Standard,* 16 Feb., 1964, p.15.

Announcement of a performance by the Syracuse Symphony, including Husa's *Portrait,* for string orchestra [W33]. Offers brief biographical information.

B524. Taber, Mark. "Music was third career choice for Czech composer-conductor." *Enquirer and News* (Battle Creek, MI), 11 Feb., 1979.

An interview with Husa, guest conductor at Albion College. "I have found that young people seem to understand my music best. . . . They have such open minds, and they are very skilled technically, too. The performances are very good."

B525. Thompson, Paul. "Husa concert: a tour de force." *Grapevine* (Ithaca), 19-25 March, 1987.

A review of an all-Husa concert by the Cornell Wind Ensemble, Cornell Glee Club and Chorus, with performances of his *Concerto,* for wind ensemble [W60]; *Concertino,* for piano and wind ensemble [W31b]; and *An American Te Deum* [W65a]. "Husa on the conductor's rostrum is an extraordinarily convincing advocate for his own music."

B526. Thoresby, Christina. "Music in France: events at Paris and Strasbourg include contributions by Americans." *Musical America* 74, (August 1954): 11.

Coverage of the Strasbourg Festival, including a brief mention of Karel Husa and his appointment to the Cornell University Faculty. Also mentions his *String quartet,* no.2 [W12], which had been recently played in a UNESCO concert in Paris.

B527. ----. "Paris notes." *Strad* 65, no.771 (July 1954): 88-89.

A report of various musical activities in Paris, including a performance of Husa's *String quartet,* no. 2 [W12]. ". . . a fine and original work, and shows that the composer has greatly matured."

B528. Tiedje, Anne. "Czech it out." *Cornell Daily Sun*, 4 Nov., 1988.

A report of the Festival of Czech Culture at Cornell University, including a performance of Husa's *Frammenti*, for organ [W6] and *String quartet*, no.3 [W16].

B529. "To honor Husa." *Ithaca Journal*, 4 Dec., 1971.

An article detailing the ceremonies and concerts presented in Husa's honor by the students and faculty at Ithaca College.

B530. Toms, John. "Risk pays off at Arkansas festival." *Tulsa Tribune*, 25 July, 1985.

A review of the opening concert of the Music Festival of Arkansas, including a performance of Husa's *Symphony no.2 "Reflections"* [W47]. "[conductor] Woods made *Reflections* . . . wholly effective and understandable. . . . where daring orchestral color and complex rhythmic patterns are more dominant than melody, Woods forged one idea into another without allowing a break in the tonal fabric."

B531. Townshend, Douglas. "New York: Verdehr Trio." *Musical America* 109, no.6 (November 1989): 46-47.

A review of a performance by the Verdehr Trio of Husa's *Sonata a tre* [W22]. ". . . the climaxes of each movement were as powerful and inevitable as those in an Elizabethan drama."

B532. "A tribute to Husa's music." *Ithaca College News*, 12 Nov., 1985, p.1+.

An announcement of the Directions in New Music Celebration at Ithaca College, honoring Husa and his contributions to music, on the occasion of his retirement from the college.

B533. Trimble, Lester. "Review: [Penderecki; Gutché; Husa]". *Stereo review* 30, no.4 (April 1973): 118.

A review of the Louisville First Edition recording [D22], including Husa's *Music for Prague, 1968* [W41]. ". . . the music on the disc is interesting . . . and in the case of Karel Husa's *Music for Prague* it is just masterly."

B534. "'Trojan women' makes its world premiere at School of Music." *Louisville Cardinal*, 27 March, 1981, p.6.

Announcement of the world premiere of Husa's ballet [W46a] at the University of Louisville, as part of the year-long celebration of the new music building on the University's Belknap campus. Includes a list of principal dancers for the work, other works to be performed on the program, and a brief biography of Husa.

B535. Trotter, Bill.   "Reviewing the year : the critics look back."   *Spectator* (Winston-Salem, NC), 14 March, 1985.

"Most intense musical experience of any kind," writes the reviewer about a performance of Husa's *Music for Prague, 1968* [W41] conducted by the composer, performed by the North Carolina School for the Arts. "Galvanized by the composer, the student orchestra delivered a searing, white-hot performance, the only performance of the year that reached the level of true cartharsis. Unforgettable."

B536. Trotter, Herman E.   "Concerto for brass quintet and string orchestra." *Buffalo Philharmonic program notes*, Feb.15, 1970: 23-25.

Notes to accompany a concert by the Buffalo Philharmonic, including a performance of Husa's *Concerto*, for brass quintet and string orchestra [W40]. "Although Karel Husa's music could have been written in no other age than our own, it differs quite dramatically from the main line of contemporary musical thought in its directness of expression and its unashamed use of the large but clear design, sonorous but rich orchestration. . . . "

B537. ----.   "Czech guest brings skills and thrills to concert."   *Buffalo Evening News*, 6 Dec., 1971.

A review of a concert by the Amherst Symphony, conducted by Husa, and including his *Music for Prague, 1968* [W41]. "In readily accessible modern scoring, with liberal use of bells and other percussion, the four movements are by turns festive, plaintive, busy and deeply spiritual. . . ."

B538. ----.   "Husa's music speaks of 20th Century with feeling for organic development." *Buffalo Evening News*, 31 Aug., 1974, p.34.

A review of available recordings of Husa's works, following a recent concert of his music in Buffalo. Includes reviews of D29, D15, D18, D22, D5, D4, D28, with an announcement of the imminent release of D3.

B539. ----.   "Karel Husa and his music of passion." *Buffalo News*, 18 March, 1979.

Article on Husa, in Buffalo to conduct the University of Buffalo Wind and

Percussion Ensembles in his *Music for Prague, 1968* [W55] and *Concerto*, for percussion and wind ensemble [W57]. "His music steadfastly insists on speaking to the heart as well as the head, and until the past few years, this has not been fashionable."

B540. ----. *"Symphony, no. 1."* *Buffalo Philharmonic program notes*, April 7, 1968: 25-26.

Notes to accompany a concert by the Buffalo Philharmonic Orchestra, conducted by Husa, and including a performance of his *Symphony, no.1* [W32]. Includes brief biographical information, and background on the composition. "The basic structure of the classical symphony is discernible, but the composer relies more on large designs and contrasts than the traditional exposition-development-recapitulation. . . ."

B541. ----. "UB Symphony Band brings small crowd to its feet." *Buffalo Evening News*, 13 May, 1974.

A review of a concert by the University of Buffalo Symphony Band, featuring a performance of Husa's *Apotheosis of this earth* [W56]. "Mr. Husa's orchestration is magnificent, radiating a fantastic panoply of cold, somber colors and building up immense, dense textures in which every element still remains clearly audible."

B542. Turok, Paul. "Tully Hall." *Music journal* 28, no.7 (September 1970): 72-73.

A review of a concert by the Fine Arts Quartet, including a performance of Husa's *String quartet, no. 3* [W16]. ". . . the easiest to listen to but by far the least interesting was Karel Husa's Pulitzer-Prize-winning *Quartet no.3.*"

B543. "Two Karels of Czech music." *Ithaca Journal*, 5 Nov., 1988.

An announcement of the first concert in Cornell University Festival of Czech Culture, featuring a performance of Husa's *Frammenti* [W6].

B544. "UWM announces Arts Festival plans." *Milwaukee Sentinel*, 27 May, 1971.

Report of the announcement of plans for the 12th annual University of Wisconsin-Milwaukee Summer Arts Festival, including Karel Husa as a guest artist, teaching 20th century music.

B545. "Vignettes : NFMC's soloists in the 1973 Holy Land tour." *Music clubs magazine* 53, no.5 (1974): 20.

A report of the world premiere of Husa's *Sonata,* for violin and piano [W17]. Includes brief information about the work and its composer.

B546. Viola, Joseph E., and Paul Wagner. "The compositions of Karel Husa." *Saxophone journal* Winter 1985: 44.

A review of the recording *Compositions of Karel Husa* [D1], including the *Concerto,* for alto saxophone and concert band [W54a], *Al fresco* [W59] and the *Concerto,* for percussion and wind ensemble [W57]. ". . . a challenging piece for both the listener and performer. . . . James Forger has recorded an excellent performance on a difficult piece. . . . This record is definitely highly recommended!"

B547. Volkmer, Fred. "Brahms birthday present." *Southampton Press* (NY), 12 May, 1983.

A review of a concert by the Long Island Chamber Ensemble, featuring works by Brahms, and including Husa's *Sonata,* no.2 for piano [W5]. "The Sonata, performed with brilliance by Mr. [Peter] Basquin, seems to stretch melody at times to the breaking point."

B548. Von Rhein, John. "CSO gives trumpet work a dazzling debut." *Chicago Tribune,* 12 Feb., 1988, sect.2, p.8.

A review of the world premiere of Husa's *Concerto,* for trumpet and orchestra [W51]. ". . . filled with prickly dissonances, terse sputters of solo virtuosity and hard, percussion-splashed timbres, . . . the score is accessible in a Central European musical idiom clearly derived from Bartok."

B549. ----. "Husa's works a living presence worldwide." *Chicago Tribune,* 12 Feb., 1988, sect.5, p.3.

An interview with Husa, prior to the world premiere of his *Concerto,* for trumpet and orchestra [W51]. ". . . my main concern has always been to create music with ideas--music that is well written, that will sound good."

B550. ----. "Leinsdorf rekindles the political drama within 'Prague 1968'." *Chicago Tribune,* 13 Dec., 1986, sect.1, p.16.

A review of a concert by the Chicago Symphony Orchestra, including works by Berlioz and Bartók, and Husa's *Music for Prague, 1968* [W41]. ". . . powerful, dramatic and disturbing; even if one listens to it as pure music, it is impossible to remain unaffected by it."

B551. Wagner, Klaus. "Vier plus vier im Hamburger 'Neuen Werk.'" *Melos: Zeitschrift für neue Musik* 29 (April 1962): 120.

A review of a concert of new music on the Norddeutschen Rundfunk, including the world premiere of Husa's *Mosaïques*, for orchestra [W38]. ". . . der stärkste Eindruck, der grösste Erfolg dieses Abends." [a powerful impression, the biggest success of the evening.]

Wagner, Paul. SEE Viola, Joseph E.

B552. Walfoort, Nina. "World premiere of 'Trojan women' ballet brings prize-winning composer to U. of L." *Louisville-Times*, 27 March, 1981, p.C1.

An interview with Husa and Alun Jones, choreographer of Husa's ballet *The Trojan women* [W46a]. The composer and choreographer discuss the inspiration for the ballet, and their collaboration on the new work for the stage, commissioned for the opening of the new music building at the University of Louisville.

B553. Weber, William. "Wind ensemble honors Sawhill." *Los Angeles Times*, 27 May, 1977, sect.IV, p.34.

A review of a concert by the UCLA Wind Ensemble, including a performance of Husa's *Concerto*, for percussion and wind ensemble [W57]. "Husa's Concerto . . . hit home hard. The row of percussionists . . . unfolded a taut, twisting chain of events. . . . One appreciated the clarity of style and the intensity of the performance."

B554. Wederich, Suzanne. "Choral performances." *American choral review* 19, no. 3 (1977): 17-18.

A report of the world permiere of Husa's *An American Te Deum* [W65a], briefly outlining the movements and texts of the work.

B555. Wetzel, Paul. "How two invasions shaped a composer's life and music." *Salt Lake Tribune*, 1 May, 1983, sect.E, p.1.

An article about Husa and the influences German and Russian invasions of Czechoslovakia had on his life and music. In a telephone interview, Husa described the composition of *Music for Prague, 1968* [W55], prior to a performance of the work by the University of Utah Symphonic Band.

B556. "What's the score: Whose fest?" *Instrumentalist* 41, no.4 (November 1986): 36.

Announcement that institutions all over the U.S. planned celebrations of Husa's 65th birthday, including the week-long *Husafest* held in Boston in December. Also notes planned performances of *Music for Prague, 1968* [W41], conducted by Eric Leinsdorf in Chicago, Philadelphia, St. Louis and Cleveland.

B557. Wierzbicki, J. "FSU's New Musical Festival: Florida State, a 'center of excellence,' proves it." *High fidelity/Musical America* 31, no.10 (October 1981): MA18-19+.

A chronicle of the FSU New Music Festival, with featured composers Ellen Taafe Zwilich and Karel Husa. Husa conducted his own *Concerto*, for percussion and wind orchestra [W57], *Concerto*, for trumpet and wind ensemble [W58a] and *Apotheosis of this earth* [W56]. ". . . each a carefully designed, meticulously paced essay in sonic density that uses a dynamically expanding tone cluster as its germinal idea."

B558. Will, Patrick T. "CCO breaks tradition with Bach and gusto." *Ithaca Journal*, 6 Dec., 1983, p.6.

A review of a performance of J.S. Bach's *Christmas oratorio*, conducted by Husa. ". . . Husa once again proved himself extraordinarily capable of marshalling unwieldy musical forces into a single, convincing unit. . . . "

B559. ----. "Once again, a triumphant and successful 'Messiah'." *Ithaca Journal*, 14 Dec., 1981, p.6.

A review of a performance by the Cayuga Chamber Orchestra and Cornell Chorale of Handel's *Messiah*, conducted by Husa. ". . . yesterday's performance had the balance of delicacy and power that only a small, well-rehearsed ensemble can provide. . . . Husa's direction was inspired and confident."

B560. Wilson, Peter. "Student orchestra wins praise on Husa's work." *Greensboro Record*, 20 July, 1971.

A review of a concert by the Eastern Symphony Orchestra at the Eastern Music Festival, conducted by Husa, and including a performance of his *Music for Prague, 1968* [W41]. "This performance was indeed an inspiring experience as Husa tried, through music, to recreate the tension in Prague during 1968."

B561. Wombell, Peter. "Oh, what a feeling--Chicago!" *Perth Sunday Times*, 6 March, 1988.

A review of a concert by the Chicago Symphony Orchestra on their Australian tour, including a performance of Husa's *Concerto*, for trumpet and orchestra [W51]. "The scoring for a big orchestra embraced some pretty spiky utterances and dissonant chords, yet it also called in some fascinating combinations of instruments . . . to provide backgrounds to the trumpet, both diffuse and ethereal."

B562. Woolsey, F.W. "Helen Starr triumphs in 'Trojan women'." *Louisville Times*, 15 February, 1985.

A review of a performance of Husa's ballet *The Trojan women* [W46a]. ". . . the score . . . growls and snarls the sounds of war with creepy authority and gives outcry to the mimed rage and sorrow of the women left in the wake of Troy's disaster."

B563. Wooten, Henry S. "Composer-conductor Husa to be at Music Festival." *Greensboro Daily News*, 18 July, 1971, p.B12.

An article announcing that Husa would be artist-in-residence for the Eastern Music Festival in Greensboro, conducting the student orchestras in his *Symphony*, no.1 [W32], *Serenade* [W39], and *Music for Prague, 1968* [W41]. Includes a brief biography with information about his education and career.

B564. ----. "Husa works are exciting; Beethoven played admirably." *Greensboro Daily News*, 23 July, 1971, p.A15.

A review of a concert performed at the 1971 Eastern Music Festival, conducted by Husa and including his *Symphony*, no.1 [W32] and *Serenade*, for woodwind quintet and orchestra [W39]. "The heavy scoring demands much from all sections of the orchestra and its musical impetus holds one's attention straight through to the dramatic crescendo which concludes the work."

B565. "World premieres." *Symphony magazine* 32, no.6 (1981): 42.

A report of the world premiere of Husa's *Trojan women* [W46a].

B566. Wyman, Max. "Symphony sparkles under Lane's baton." *Vancouver Sun*, 29 Nov., 1971, p.38.

A review of a concert by the Vancouver Symphony Orchestra, including a performance of Husa's *Music for Prague, 1968* [W41]. ". . . a magnificently structured and very moving piece that deploys the resources of the orchestra to unusual and fierce effect."

B567. Young, Julie Ann. "Music for Prague 1968: a symbolic analysis." *Triangle of Mu Phi Epsilon* 81, no.2 (1986-87): 4-5.

An excerpt of a paper which won first place in the 1986 Mu Phi Epsilon musicological research contest (category 4, Undergraduate research papers). In this paper, the author identifies the "many passages which were meant by the composer to be symbolic of something specific" in Husa's *Music for Prague, 1968* [W41].

B568. Zakariasen, Bill. "Off the beaten path--and into glory." *New York Daily News*, 9 May, 1989, p.51.

A review of a concert by the New York Philharmonic, including a performance of Husa's *Music for Prague, 1968* [W41]. ". . . a deeply moving musical experience . . . "

B569. ----. "They followed his lead." *New York Daily News*, 27 Sept., 1986.

A review of a concert by the New York Philharmonic, including the world premiere of Husa's *Concerto*, for orchestra [W49]. ". . . Husa has strong musical ideas and isn't afraid of using the grand gesture to express and develop them."

B570. Zuck, Barbara. "Karel Husa wants his music to speak for today." *Columbus Dispatch*, 23 March, 1984, p.C13.

An interview with Husa, visiting the Capitol University Conservatory of Music. Includes brief biographical information, and Husa's thoughts on the acceptance of contemporary music.

Appendix A: Alphabetical List of Compositions

Numbers following each title, e.g., W40, refer to the "Works and Performances" section of this volume.

Al fresco, for band, W59
An American Te Deum, for baritone solo, mixed chorus and wind ensemble, W65a
An American Te Deum, for baritone solo, mixed chorus and orchestra, W65b
Apotheosis of this earth, for band, W56
Apotheosis of this earth, for chorus and orchestra, W64

Cantata, for male chorus and brass quintet, W68
Concertino, for piano and orchestra, W31a
Concertino, for piano and wind ensemble, W31b
Concerto, for alto saxophone and band, W53a
Concerto, for alto saxophone and piano, W53a
Concerto, for brass quintet and string orchestra, W40
Concerto, for orchestra, W49
Concerto, for organ and orchestra, W50
Concerto, for percussion and wind ensemble, W57
Concerto, for trumpet and orchestra, W51
Concerto, for trumpet and piano, W58b
Concerto, for trumpet and wind orchestra, W58a
Concerto, for violoncello and orchestra, W52
Concerto, for wind ensemble, W60
Czech duets, for piano (4 hands), W3

Dance sketches, W19
Divertimento, for brass ensemble and percussion, W13a

Divertimento, for brass quintet, W13b
Divertimento, for string orchestra, W30

Eight Czech duets SEE Czech duets
Elegie, for piano, W4
Elegie et rondeau, for saxophone and orchestra, W37
Elegie et rondeau, for saxophone and piano, W14
Every day, for mixed chorus a cappella, W67
Evocations de Slovaquie, W11

Fanfare, for brass ensemble and percussion, W21
Fantasies, for orchestra, W35
Festive ode, for mixed chorus and orchestra, W63
Four little pieces SEE Little pieces
Frammenti, for organ, W6
Fresque, for orchestra, W29b
Fresques, for orchestra, W29a

Intrada, for brass quintet, W25
Intradas and interludes, for 7 trumpets and percussion, W20

Landscapes, for brass quintet, W18
Little pieces, for strings, W34

Monodrama, portrait of an artist, ballet, W44
Moravian songs, for mixed chorus a cappella, W66
Moravian songs, for voice and piano, W62
Mosaïques, for orchestra, W38
Music for Prague, for band, W55
Music for Prague, for orchestra, W41
Musique d'amateurs, for orchestra, W53b
Musique pour harmonie, for winds and percussion, W53a

Overture, for orchestra, W27

Pastoral, for string orchestra, W45
Poem, for viola and chamber orchestra, W36
Portrait, for string orchestra, W33
Preludes, W15

Recollections, for woodwind quintet and piano, W23
Reflections SEE Symphony, no. 2, for orchestra

Serenade, for woodwind quintet, string, harp and xylophone, W39
Sinfonietta, for orchestra, W28
Smetana fanfare, for band, W61
Sonata a tre, for violin, clarinet and piano, W22
Sonata, for violin and piano, W17
Sonata, no. 1, for piano, W2
Sonata, no. 2, for piano, W5

Sonatina, for piano, W1
Sonatina, for violin and piano, W9
Sonnets by Michelangelo, W42
Steadfast tin soldier, W43
String quartet, W7
String quartet, no. 1, W10
String quartet, no. 2, W12
String quartet, no. 3, W16
String quartet, no. 4, W26
Suite, for viola and piano, W8
Symphonic suite, for orchestra, W48
Symphony, no. 1, for orchestra, W32
Symphony, no. 2, for orchestra, W47

There are from time to time mornings, for mixed chorus a cappella, W65c
Three dance sketches SEE Dance sketches
Three fresques SEE Fresques
Three Moravian songs SEE Moravian songs
The Trojan women, ballet, W46a
The Trojan women, suite, W46b
Twelve Moravian songs SEE Moravian songs
Two preludes SEE Preludes
Two sonnets by Michelangelo SEE Sonnets by Michelangelo

Variations, for violin, viola, violoncello and piano, W24

Appendix B: Chronological List of Compositions

Numbers following each title, e.g., W40, refer to the "Works and Performances" section of this volume.

1943	Sonatina, for piano, W1 String quartet, W7
1944	Overture, for orchestra, W27 Sinfonietta, for orchestra, W28
1945	Suite, for viola and piano, W8 Sonatina, for violin and piano, W9
1947	Three fresques, for orchestra, W29a
1948	String quartet, no. 1, W10 Divertimento, for string orchestra, W30
1949	Sonata, no. 1, for piano, W2 Concertino, for piano and orchestra, W31a
1951	Evocations de Slovaquie, for clarinet, viola and violoncello, W11 Musique pour harmonie, for winds and percussion, W53a
1953	Symphony, no. 1, for orchestra, W32 Portrait, for string orchestra, W33 Musique d'amateurs, for orchestra, W53b String quartet, no. 2, W12

1955   Eight Czech duets, for piano (4 hands), W3
        Four little pieces, for strings, W34

1956   Fantasies, for orchestra, W35
        Twelve Moravian songs, for voice and piano, W62

1957   Elegie, for piano, W4

1958   Divertimento, for brass and percussion, W13a

1959   Poem, for viola and chamber orchestra, W36

1960   Elegie et rondeau, for saxophone and piano, W14

1961   Elegie et rondeau, for saxophone and orchestra, W37
        Mosaïques, for orchestra, W38

1963   Fresque, for orchestra, W29b
        Serenade, for woodwind quintet, strings, harp and xylophone, W39

1964   Festive ode, for chorus and orchestra, W63

1965   Concerto, for brass quintet and string orchestra, W40

1966   Two preludes, for flute, clarinet and bassoon, W15

1967   Concerto, for alto saxophone and conert band, W53a

1968   String quartet, no. 3, W16
        Divertimento, for brass quintet, W13b
        Music for Prague, 1968, for band, W55

1969   Music for Prague, 1968, for orchestra, W41

1970   Apotheosis of this earth, for concert band, W56

1971   Concerto, for percussion and wind ensemble, W57
        Two sonnets by Michelangelo, for orchestra, W42

1972   Concerto, for alto saxophone and piano, W53b
        Apotheosis of this earth, for chorus and orchestra, W64

1973   Sonata, for violin and piano, W1
        Concerto, for trumpet and wind orchestra, W58a

1974   Al fresco, for band, W59
        The steadfast tin soldier, for narrator and orchestra, W43

1975   Sonata, no. 2, for piano, W5

1976   An American Te Deum, for baritone solo, chorus and wind
        ensemble, W65a
        Concerto, for trumpet and piano, W58b
        Monodrama, ballet, for orchestra, W44
        There are from time to time mornings, for mixed chorus a cappella,
        W65c

1977   An American Te Deum, for baritone solo, chorus and orchestra,
        W65b
        Landscapes, for brass quintet, W18

1979   Three dance sketches, for percussion, W19
        Pastoral, for string orchestra, W45

1980   Intradas and interludes, for 7 trumpets and percussion, W20
        The Trojan women, ballet, for orchestra, W46a

1981   Fanfare, for brass ensemble and percussion, W21
        Three Moravian songs, for mixed chorus a cappella, W66
        Every day, for mixed chorus a cappella, W67
        Sonata a tre, for violin, clarinet and piano, W22

1982   Recollections, for woodwind quintet and piano, W23
        Concerto, for wind ensemble, W60
        Cantata, for male chorus and brass quintet, W68

1983   Concertino, for piano and wind ensemble, W31b
        Symphony, no. 2, "Reflections", for orchestra, W47

1984   The Trojan women, suite, for orchestra, W46b
        Smetana fanfare, for band, W61
        Variations, for violin, viola, violoncello and piano, W24
        Symphonic suite, for orchestra, W48
        Intrada, for brass quintet, W25

1986   Concerto, for orchestra, W49

1987   Concerto, for organ and orchestra, W50
        Concerto, for trumpet and orchestra, W51
        Frammenti, for organ, W6

1988   Concerto, for violoncello and orchestra, W52
        Evocations de Slovaquie, W11b

In progress   String quartet, no. 4, W26
              Concerto, for violin and orchestra [no work number]

Index

Page numbers, e.g., p.5, refer to pages in the "Biography"; numbers preceded by a "B" refer to the "Bibliography"; numbers preceded by a "D" refer to the "Discography"; numbers preceded by a "W" refer to the "Works and Performances" section.

About the Author

SUSAN HAYES HITCHENS is Music Librarian at the University of Kansas.